Touchdown JUMBLE®

Tackle These Peerless Puzzles!

Henri Arnold,
Bob Lee,
Mike Argirion,
Jeff Knurek, &
David L. Hoyt

TRIUMPH
BOOKS

This book is available in quantity at special discounts
for your group or organization.

For further information, contact:

Triumph Books LLC
814 North Franklin Street
Chicago, Illinois 60610
Phone: (312) 337-0747
www.triumphbooks.com

Printed in U.S.A.

ISBN: 978-1-62937-212-9

Design by Sue Knopf

Contents

Touchdown JUMBLE®

CLASSIC PUZZLES

PUZZLE 1

JUMBLE®

Unscramble these four Jumbles, one letter to each square, to form four ordinary words.

COASH

MYLAN

VILEWE

GURFEE

DPT... EAL... ALS... RXP... DTL..
23 1/4 ... 17 1/2 ... 20 7/8 ... 78 1/2 ... 24
$
WHAT SOME SO-CALLED "GOOD BUYS" IN WALL STREET OFTEN TURN OUT TO BE.

Now arrange the circled letters to form the surprise answer, as suggested by the above cartoon.

Print answer here " "

JUMBLE®

Unscramble these four Jumbles, one letter to each square, to form four ordinary words.

CATEX

GEDEW

NORZEF

VITANY

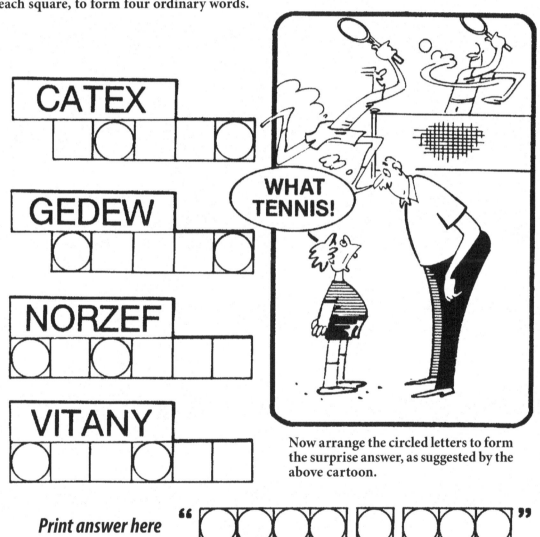

Now arrange the circled letters to form the surprise answer, as suggested by the above cartoon.

Print answer here " ◯◯◯◯ ◯ ◯◯◯ "

PUZZLE 3

JUMBLE®

Unscramble these four Jumbles, one letter to each square, to form four ordinary words.

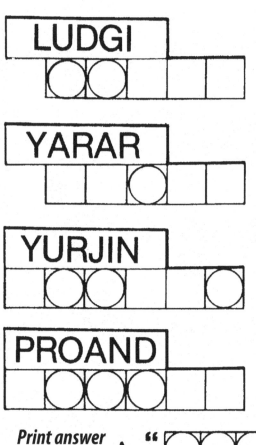

LUDGI

YARAR

YURJIN

PROAND

WHAT HE CALLED THOSE PEOPLE WHO ACQUITTED HIM.

Now arrange the circled letters to form the surprise answer, as suggested by the above cartoon.

Print answer here A " "

PUZZLE 4

JUMBLE®

Unscramble these four Jumbles, one letter to each square, to form four ordinary words.

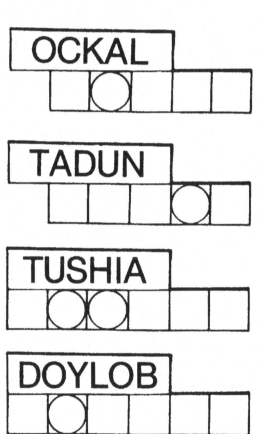

OCKAL

TADUN

TUSHIA

DOYLOB

HOW YOU SOMETIMES END UP IF YOU GO ALL OUT.

Now arrange the circled letters to form the surprise answer, as suggested by the above cartoon.

Print answer here

PUZZLE 5

JUMBLE®

Unscramble these four Jumbles, one letter to each square, to form four ordinary words.

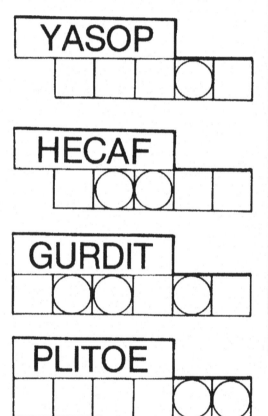

YASOP

HECAF

GURDIT

PLITOE

ALL FLIGHTS TEMPORARILY DELAYED
GATE 2
GATE 4

WHAT WERE THE PROSPECTS OF DEPARTURE DURING THE BIG BLIZZARD?

Now arrange the circled letters to form the surprise answer, as suggested by the above cartoon.

Print answer here ☐☐ IN ☐☐☐☐ ☐☐☐☐

JUMBLE®

Unscramble these four Jumbles, one letter to each square, to form four ordinary words.

ELZAH

UBOAT

BONGIB

SEEBID

WHIR-R-R-R
THE WHEEL WAS CONSIDERED MAN'S GREATEST INVENTION UNTIL HE GOT THIS.

Now arrange the circled letters to form the surprise answer, as suggested by the above cartoon.

Print answer here

PUZZLE 7

JUMBLE®

Unscramble these four Jumbles, one letter to each square, to form four ordinary words.

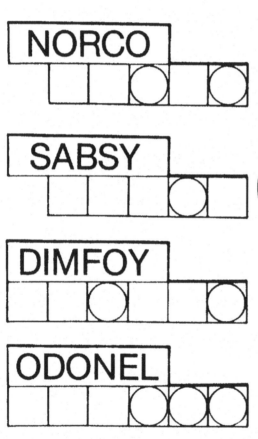

NORCO

SABSY

DIMFOY

ODONEL

And just yesterday it was so cold
HOW SPRING OFTEN ARRIVES.

Now arrange the circled letters to form the surprise answer, as suggested by the above cartoon.

Print answer here " - "

PUZZLE 8

JUMBLE®

Unscramble these four Jumbles, one letter to each square, to form four ordinary words.

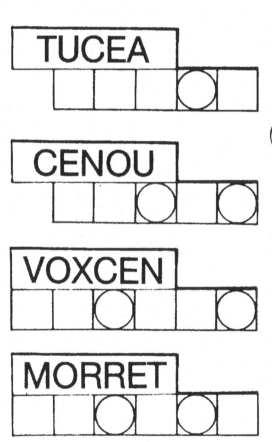

TUCEA

CENOU

VOXCEN

MORRET

Psst—you'd better see your friend home
WHAT HIS FAVORITE DRINK WAS.

Now arrange the circled letters to form the surprise answer, as suggested by the above cartoon.

Print answer here THE

JUMBLE®

Unscramble these four Jumbles, one letter to each square, to form four ordinary words.

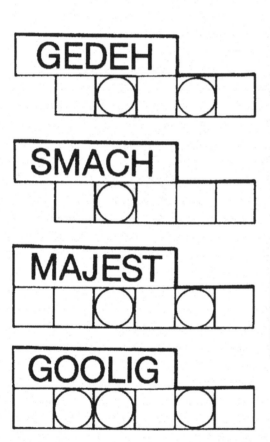

GEDEH

SMACH

MAJEST

GOOLIG

Never felt better
Wish I felt as young as he does
THE BIRTHDAY CAKE HAD SO MANY CANDLES ON IT SO HE COULD MAKE THIS.

Now arrange the circled letters to form the surprise answer, as suggested by the above cartoon.

Print answer here ☐☐☐☐☐ OF HIS ☐☐☐

PUZZLE 10

JUMBLE®

Unscramble these four Jumbles, one letter to each square, to form four ordinary words.

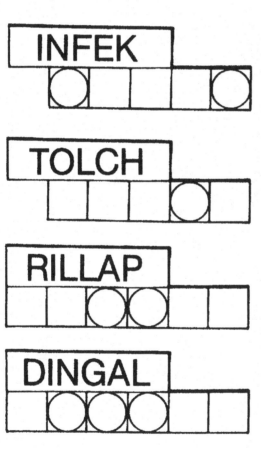

INFEK

TOLCH

RILLAP

DINGAL

a–e
f–k
l–p
YAK YAK
YAK YAK
WHAT THERE WAS A LOT OF AT THE EMPLOYMENT AGENCY.

Now arrange the circled letters to form the surprise answer, as suggested by the above cartoon.

Print answer here “ ”

PUZZLE 11

JUMBLE®

Unscramble these four Jumbles, one letter to each square, to form four ordinary words.

WOSOP

YEJON

UNPOCE

TIQUEY

WHAT A YOUNG MAN OFTEN HAS TO DO AFTER DECIDING TO POP THE QUESTION.

Now arrange the circled letters to form the surprise answer, as suggested by the above cartoon.

Print answer here ◯◯◯◯◯◯◯◯ THE ◯◯◯

JUMBLE®

Unscramble these four Jumbles, one letter to each square, to form four ordinary words.

ZOPAT

YELCC

RESOOM

RATTUN

And they were supposed to be the favorites
WHAT THE LOSING TEAM WAS WHEN THERE WAS AN UPSET IN THE BALLGAME.

Now arrange the circled letters to form the surprise answer, as suggested by the above cartoon.

Print answer here

JUMBLE®

Unscramble these four Jumbles, one letter to each square, to form four ordinary words.

MOPET

PHEES

YOTHER

BELTOT

WHAT ALL THOSE SUGGESTIONS ABOUT IMPROVING THE DOUGHNUT BUSINESS SEEMED TO HAVE.

Now arrange the circled letters to form the surprise answer, as suggested by the above cartoon.

Print answer here IN

PUZZLE 14

JUMBLE®

Unscramble these four Jumbles, one letter to each square, to form four ordinary words.

RAUZE

BETER

SURWAL

INGROI

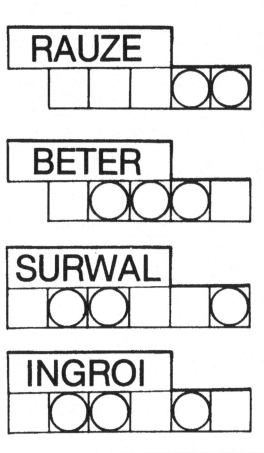

There goes his promotion
SOME PEOPLE MIGHT RISE HIGHER IF THEY'D LEARN TO DO THIS.

Now arrange the circled letters to form the surprise answer, as suggested by the above cartoon.

Print answer here

JUMBLE®

Unscramble these four Jumbles, one letter to each square, to form four ordinary words.

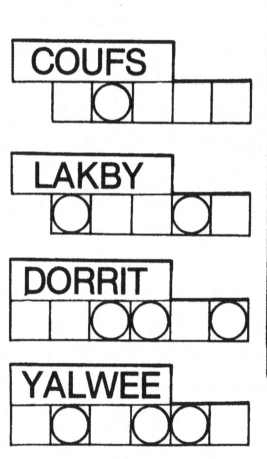

COUFS

LAKBY

DORRIT

YALWEE

Sorry, I've changed my mind
PRIVATE
DICTIO-NARY
WHAT A HYPHEN PERMITS YOU TO DO.

Now arrange the circled letters to form the surprise answer, as suggested by the above cartoon.

Print answer here ◯◯◯◯◯ YOUR ◯◯◯◯

PUZZLE 16

JUMBLE®

Unscramble these four Jumbles, one letter to each square, to form four ordinary words.

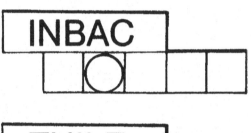

INBAC

THILE

PLOGES

REPHEL

Er-ah-er, d-do y-you
l-love me?

ONE ISN'T SURE TO SAY IT.

Now arrange the circled letters to form the surprise answer, as suggested by the above cartoon.

Print answer here

JUMBLE®

Unscramble these four Jumbles, one letter to each square, to form four ordinary words.

LICCO

ORFID

BONKER

APHERM

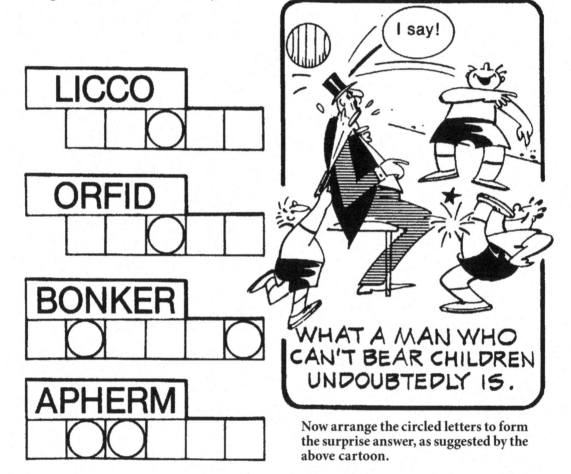

I say!
WHAT A MAN WHO CAN'T BEAR CHILDREN UNDOUBTEDLY IS.

Now arrange the circled letters to form the surprise answer, as suggested by the above cartoon.

Print answer here

PUZZLE 18

JUMBLE®

Unscramble these four Jumbles, one letter to each square, to form four ordinary words.

ROGOM

FUTOL

SINVIO

NAHLED

He's cheated everyone he's ever met
WHAT HE WAS DOING TIME FOR.

Now arrange the circled letters to form the surprise answer, as suggested by the above cartoon.

Print answer here " "

JUMBLE®

Unscramble these four Jumbles, one letter to each square, to form four ordinary words.

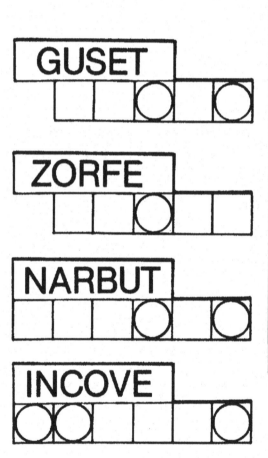

GUSET

ZORFE

NARBUT

INCOVE

A MAN WITH HORSE SENSE SHOULD KNOW ENOUGH NOT TO DO THIS.

Now arrange the circled letters to form the surprise answer, as suggested by the above cartoon.

Print answer here

PUZZLE 20

JUMBLE®

Unscramble these four Jumbles, one letter to each square, to form four ordinary words.

PIMBL

VAMUE

REPOPH

BISMUT

WHAT THOSE TWINS WERE AS ALIKE AS.

Now arrange the circled letters to form the surprise answer, as suggested by the above cartoon.

Print answer here " ◯◯◯ - ◯◯◯◯◯ "

PUZZLE 21

JUMBLE®

Unscramble these four Jumbles, one letter to each square, to form four ordinary words.

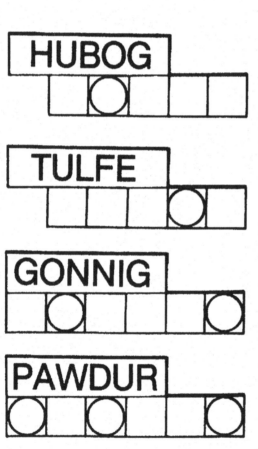

HUBOG

TULFE

GONNIG

PAWDUR

HOW THE ASTRONAUT'S WIFE WAS ALWAYS HAPPY TO SEE HIM.

Now arrange the circled letters to form the surprise answer, as suggested by the above cartoon.

Print answer here " & "

PUZZLE 22

JUMBLE®

Unscramble these four Jumbles, one letter to each square, to form four ordinary words.

RIDUL

PYNOH

TEWPER

GOFERR

WHAT THAT LITTLE FLOOR COVERING WAS.

Now arrange the circled letters to form the surprise answer, as suggested by the above cartoon.

Print answer here A " "

PUZZLE 23

JUMBLE®

Unscramble these four Jumbles, one letter to each square, to form four ordinary words.

LAVNA

GIJON

ENBODY

FEANED

PEOPLE WHO ARE ALWAYS FLYING INTO A RAGE SOMETIMES END UP MAKING THIS.

Now arrange the circled letters to form the surprise answer, as suggested by the above cartoon.

Print answer here A

PUZZLE 24

JUMBLE®

Unscramble these four Jumbles, one letter to each square, to form four ordinary words.

YAIDS

MEFAL

RATVAC

MYSALE

WHAT A PRACTICAL JOKER DOES.

Now arrange the circled letters to form the surprise answer, as suggested by the above cartoon.

Print answer here TO

PUZZLE 25

JUMBLE®

Unscramble these four Jumbles, one letter to each square, to form four ordinary words.

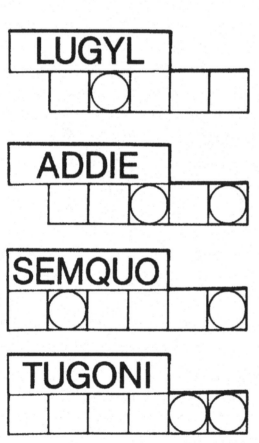

LUGYL

ADDIE

SEMQUO

TUGONI

I'm not putting up with this!

HOW THE OLD CURMUDGEON STALKED OUT OF THAT RESTAURANT.

Now arrange the circled letters to form the surprise answer, as suggested by the above cartoon.

Print answer here IN A

Touchdown JUMBLE®

DAILY

PUZZLES

PUZZLE 26

JUMBLE®

Unscramble these four Jumbles, one letter to each square, to form four ordinary words.

NACAL

ABDEK

TASSID

COHMER

WHAT THEY CALL SOME OF THOSE MEN WHO RUN THE GAMING TABLES.

Now arrange the circled letters to form the surprise answer, as suggested by the above cartoon.

Print answer here " "

JUMBLE®

Unscramble these four Jumbles, one letter to each square, to form four ordinary words.

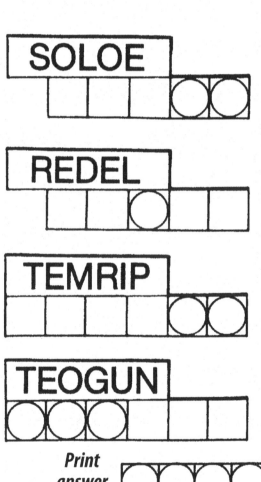

SOLOE

REDEL

TEMRIP

TEOGUN

Doesn't believe in having any fun
WHAT AN INHIBITED PERSON USUALLY IS.

Now arrange the circled letters to form the surprise answer, as suggested by the above cartoon.

Print answer here UP IN " "

JUMBLE®

Unscramble these four Jumbles, one letter to each square, to form four ordinary words.

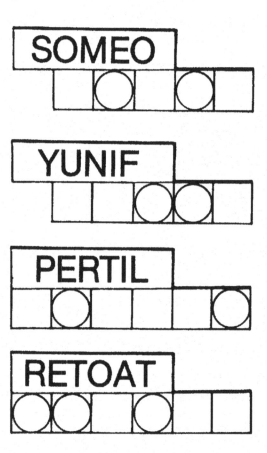

SOMEO

YUNIF

PERTIL

RETOAT

WHAT SOME SPEAKERS DO WHEN GIVEN THE FLOOR.

Now arrange the circled letters to form the surprise answer, as suggested by the above cartoon.

Print answer here ◯◯◯◯◯ THE ◯◯◯◯

PUZZLE
29

JUMBLE®

Unscramble these four Jumbles, one letter to each square, to form four ordinary words.

WORNC

DISAT

LEGBIT

TELMAD

I wouldn't go out with a guy who looks like that
A MIDDLE-AGE SPREAD IS SIMPLY THIS.

Now arrange the circled letters to form the surprise answer, as suggested by the above cartoon.

Print answer here A ______ OF _____

JUMBLE®

Unscramble these four Jumbles, one letter to each square, to form four ordinary words.

YABBE

THRAW

YECKAL

ACTUFE

He should hit the books more often
F
WHAT THE HALFBACK WAS IN HIS CLASSROOM WORK.

Now arrange the circled letters to form the surprise answer, as suggested by the above cartoon.

Print answer here

PUZZLE 31

JUMBLE®

Unscramble these four Jumbles, one letter to each square, to form four ordinary words.

CARPH

TIBEF

JOOSUY

GURDED

WHEN IT COMES TO LOVE, AN ENGAGEMENT RING IS USUALLY JUST THIS.

Now arrange the circled letters to form the surprise answer, as suggested by the above cartoon.

Print answer here A "◯◯◯" ◯◯◯◯◯◯◯

JUMBLE®

Unscramble these four Jumbles, one letter to each square, to form four ordinary words.

KNITH

OAKEW

CEDROF

GOEMAH

SOME GUYS DON'T KNOW WHEN TO STOP UNTIL THEY'RE TOLD THIS.

Now arrange the circled letters to form the surprise answer, as suggested by the above cartoon.

Print answer here

PUZZLE 33

JUMBLE®

Unscramble these four Jumbles, one letter to each square, to form four ordinary words.

AGMOD

HOPAC

LEWFOL

RETANB

WHAT A YAWN OFTEN IS.

Now arrange the circled letters to form the surprise answer, as suggested by the above cartoon.

Print answer here A ◯◯◯◯ MADE BY A ◯◯◯◯

PUZZLE 34

JUMBLE®

Unscramble these four Jumbles, one letter to each square, to form four ordinary words.

WHAT THE BLACK-SMITH DID TO HIS INCOMPETENT APPRENTICE.

WILEH

DABIE

KLEACT

DROOVE

Now arrange the circled letters to form the surprise answer, as suggested by the above cartoon.

Print answer here HIM

JUMBLE®

Unscramble these four Jumbles, one letter to each square, to form four ordinary words.

VERIP

OAQUT

KUSTEM

DEGLUC

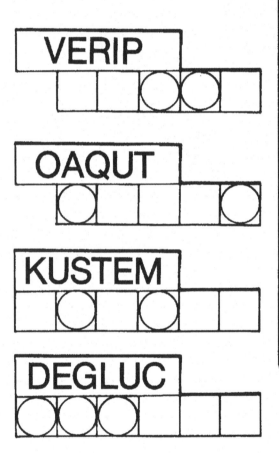

Cures bunions, baldness, athlete's foot. . .
MEDICINE MEN ARE SELDOM WHAT THEY'RE THIS.

Now arrange the circled letters to form the surprise answer, as suggested by the above cartoon.

Print answer here " " TO BE

PUZZLE 36

JUMBLE®

Unscramble these four Jumbles, one letter to each square, to form four ordinary words.

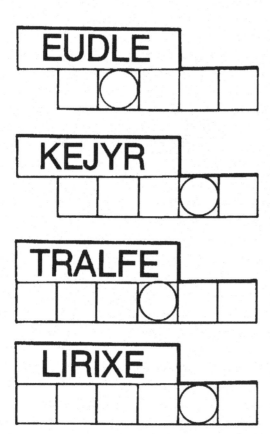

EUDLE

KEJYR

TRALFE

LIRIXE

WHAT THE SCOTSMAN WHO RETURNED HOME LATE ONE NIGHT ALMOST GOT.

Now arrange the circled letters to form the surprise answer, as suggested by the above cartoon.

Print answer here “ ”

PUZZLE 37

JUMBLE®

Unscramble these four Jumbles, one letter to each square, to form four ordinary words.

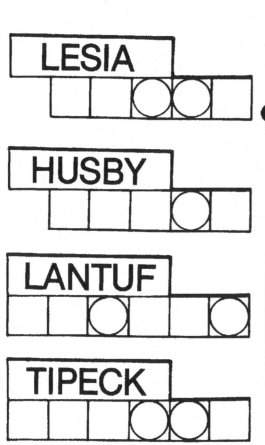

LESIA

HUSBY

LANTUF

TIPECK

THOSE CARS NEVER RUN AS SMOOTHLY AS THIS.

Now arrange the circled letters to form the surprise answer, as suggested by the above cartoon.

Print answer here

Unscramble these four Jumbles, one letter to each square, to form four ordinary words.

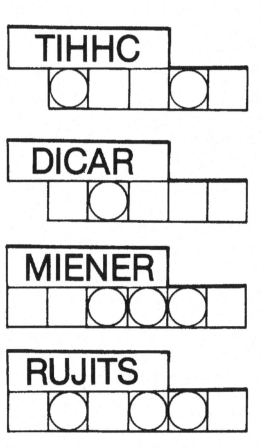

TIHHC

DICAR

MIENER

RUJITS

WHAT THE VIOLINIST WAS UP TO.

Now arrange the circled letters to form the surprise answer, as suggested by the above cartoon.

Print answer here HIS ⬡⬡⬡⬡ IN ⬡⬡⬡⬡⬡

PUZZLE 39

JUMBLE®

Unscramble these four Jumbles, one letter to each square, to form four ordinary words.

KAWTE

ROJEK

TULTER

EMPAND

First fill these out in triplicate
Then take them to. . .
APPLICATIONS ACCEPTED HERE
WHAT A BUREAUCRAT IS.

Now arrange the circled letters to form the surprise answer, as suggested by the above cartoon.

Print answer here A

PUZZLE 40

JUMBLE®

Unscramble these four Jumbles, one letter to each square, to form four ordinary words.

MUJYP

NAPOR

DRENER

NAMMAD

For once I played like a pro

WHAT THE GOLF ADDICT'S CHILDREN CALLED THEIR FATHER.

Now arrange the circled letters to form the surprise answer, as suggested by the above cartoon.

Print answer here " - "

JUMBLE®

Unscramble these four Jumbles, one letter to each square, to form four ordinary words.

SKUYD

VALIT

FLORGE

DUQILI

WHY HE NEVER GOT TIRED OF PROPOSING MARRIAGE TO THE MOONSHINER.

Now arrange the circled letters to form the surprise answer, as suggested by the above cartoon.

Print answer here HE ○○○○○ HER ○○○○○

PUZZLE 42

JUMBLE®

Unscramble these four Jumbles, one letter to each square, to form four ordinary words.

TAHBE

KROPE

RUQUOM

TUCSOC

Missed again!
WHAT A DUCK HUNTER MIGHT BE.

Now arrange the circled letters to form the surprise answer, as suggested by the above cartoon.

Print answer here A " "

PUZZLE 43

JUMBLE®

Unscramble these four Jumbles, one letter to each square, to form four ordinary words.

ELBIG

INFAL

SHRUPE

LAIHNE

He's going far
Ugh!
HE STOOPS LOW BECAUSE HE'S ANXIOUS TO DO THIS.

Now arrange the circled letters to form the surprise answer, as suggested by the above cartoon.

Print answer here

PUZZLE 44

JUMBLE®

Unscramble these four Jumbles, one letter to each square, to form four ordinary words.

LERIN

SILAA

WALLUF

HESTOO

WHAT JOKES TOLD BY MOUNTAIN FOLK OFTEN ARE.

Now arrange the circled letters to form the surprise answer, as suggested by the above cartoon.

Print answer here " - "

PUZZLE 45

JUMBLE®

Unscramble these four Jumbles, one letter to each square, to form four ordinary words.

PETIR

BYGAG

YEWARL

BOIPHS

HAPPY NEW YEAR
WHAT TODAY'S HANGOVER MIGHT BE CONNECTED WITH.

Now arrange the circled letters to form the surprise answer, as suggested by the above cartoon.

Print answer here THE ○○○○○ OF ○○○○○○

PUZZLE 46

JUMBLE®

Unscramble these four Jumbles, one letter to each square, to form four ordinary words.

LEXIE

TENGA

DISTOL

SNOPER

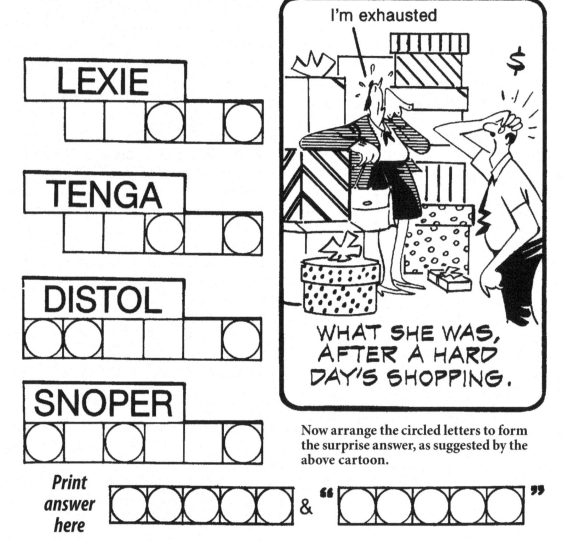

I'm exhausted
$
WHAT SHE WAS, AFTER A HARD DAY'S SHOPPING.

Now arrange the circled letters to form the surprise answer, as suggested by the above cartoon.

Print answer here ☐☐☐☐☐ & "☐☐☐☐☐"

PUZZLE
47

JUMBLE®

Unscramble these four Jumbles, one letter to each square, to form four ordinary words.

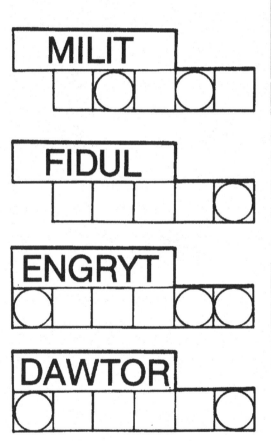

MILIT

FIDUL

ENGRYT

DAWTOR

I always speak my mind
WHAT A PERSON WHO CALLS A SPADE A SPADE IS PROBABLY ABOUT TO GIVE SOMEONE.

Now arrange the circled letters to form the surprise answer, as suggested by the above cartoon.

Print answer here A ______ " ___ "

JUMBLE®

Unscramble these four Jumbles, one letter to each square, to form four ordinary words.

SEECA

TIFAH

CURPES

HATTUG

If you stop doing that, you'll get your bike!

WHAT'S THE BEST THING FOR NAIL-BITING?

Now arrange the circled letters to form the surprise answer, as suggested by the above cartoon.

Print answer here

JUMBLE®

Unscramble these four Jumbles, one letter to each square, to form four ordinary words.

RATAL

DAMAR

ANNICE

MEEPID

WHAT GETTING RID OF HER MAIDEN NAME WAS.

Now arrange the circled letters to form the surprise answer, as suggested by the above cartoon.

Print answer here HER

JUMBLE®

Unscramble these four Jumbles, one letter to each square, to form four ordinary words.

LUNNA

CAWAM

FEEGUR

RAGETT

WHAT'S THE BEST LOOKING FIGURE IN GEOMETRY?

Now arrange the circled letters to form the surprise answer, as suggested by the above cartoon.

Print answer here " - "

PUZZLE 51

JUMBLE®

Unscramble these four Jumbles, one letter to each square, to form four ordinary words.

YEAPE

ARSYC

BLIMEN

DROICH

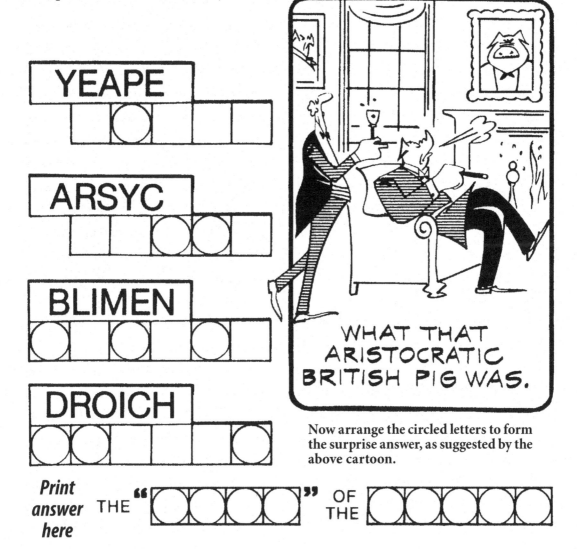

WHAT THAT ARISTOCRATIC BRITISH PIG WAS.

Now arrange the circled letters to form the surprise answer, as suggested by the above cartoon.

Print answer here THE "◯◯◯◯" OF THE ◯◯◯◯◯◯

PUZZLE 52

JUMBLE®

Unscramble these four Jumbles, one letter to each square, to form four ordinary words.

KLULS

ORVAB

GWEEDD

NAMALY

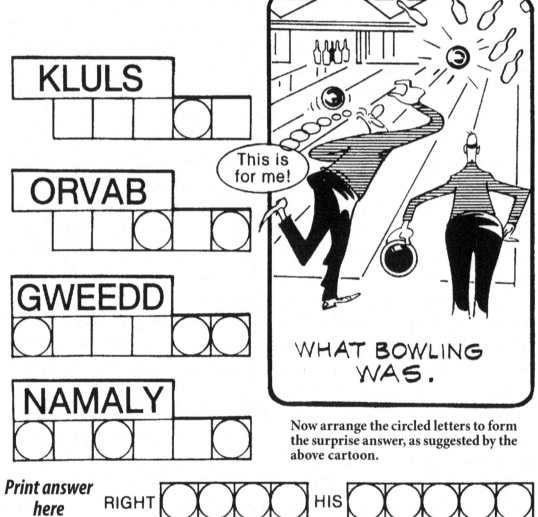

This is for me!
WHAT BOWLING WAS.

Now arrange the circled letters to form the surprise answer, as suggested by the above cartoon.

Print answer here RIGHT ◯◯◯◯ HIS ◯◯◯◯◯

PUZZLE
53

JUMBLE®

Unscramble these four Jumbles, one letter to each square, to form four ordinary words.

YANON

ROCCU

PIRAMI

TERROM

That will be two dollars
WHAT WEDDING FEES USUALLY AMOUNT TO.

Now arrange the circled letters to form the surprise answer, as suggested by the above cartoon.

Print answer here THE "   "

PUZZLE 54

JUMBLE®

Unscramble these four Jumbles, one letter to each square, to form four ordinary words.

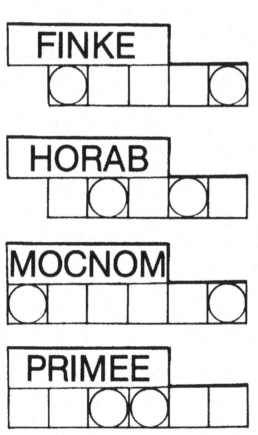

FINKE

HORAB

MOCNOM

PRIMEE

He's easy to get along with
WHAT THE PEACEFUL VEGETARIAN WAS NEVER ABOUT TO DO WITH ANYONE.

Now arrange the circled letters to form the surprise answer, as suggested by the above cartoon.

Print answer here ◯◯◯◯ A ◯◯◯◯

JUMBLE®

Unscramble these four Jumbles, one letter to each square, to form four ordinary words.

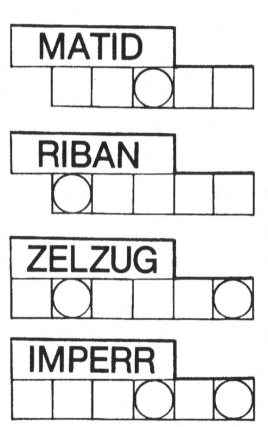

MATID

RIBAN

ZELZUG

IMPERR

THE JOKE TOLD BY THE TRAMP TURNED OUT TO BE THIS.

Now arrange the circled letters to form the surprise answer, as suggested by the above cartoon.

Print answer here A " "

PUZZLE 56

JUMBLE®

Unscramble these four Jumbles, one letter to each square, to form four ordinary words.

SITOC

ZYZUF

DAIMWY

BRAGLE

Don't know what we'd do without him

WHAT A MAN WITH A "BURNING" AMBITION IS NOT APT TO GET.

Now arrange the circled letters to form the surprise answer, as suggested by the above cartoon.

Print answer here " "

JUMBLE®

Unscramble these four Jumbles, one letter to each square, to form four ordinary words.

LEEBI

DATUC

CHARNB

GLENET

Oops!
STUDENT DRIVER
HOW SOME PEOPLE LEARN TO DRIVE A CAR.

Now arrange the circled letters to form the surprise answer, as suggested by the above cartoon.

Print answer here BY

PUZZLE 58

JUMBLE®

Unscramble these four Jumbles, one letter to each square, to form four ordinary words.

TROFY

LAHCK

CODEED

PERTAT

WHAT THAT
WELL-TO-DO
MAN WAS.

Now arrange the circled letters to form the surprise answer, as suggested by the above cartoon.

Print answer here ☐☐☐☐ ☐☐ "☐☐"

PUZZLE 59

JUMBLE®

Unscramble these four Jumbles, one letter to each square, to form four ordinary words.

TRYNE

FLUTA

ENFADE

SMIBUT

HOW HE SEEMED TO BE GOING TO SCHOOL.

Now arrange the circled letters to form the surprise answer, as suggested by the above cartoon.

Print answer here " "

PUZZLE 60

JUMBLE®

Unscramble these four Jumbles, one letter to each square, to form four ordinary words.

GUPER

HUGAL

QUEETA

SUTTOM

Are you aware of the seriousness of the charges against you?
WHAT THAT SUCCESSFUL CRIMINAL WAS.

Now arrange the circled letters to form the surprise answer, as suggested by the above cartoon.

Print answer here A

PUZZLE 61

JUMBLE®

Unscramble these four Jumbles, one letter to each square, to form four ordinary words.

CHELE

RAHME

PARULL

FAIRAS

I submit that my client is not responsible for his actions
A KLEPTOMANIAC "HELPS HIMSELF" BECAUSE HE CAN'T DO THIS.

Now arrange the circled letters to form the surprise answer, as suggested by the above cartoon.

Print answer here

PUZZLE 62

JUMBLE®

Unscramble these four Jumbles, one letter to each square, to form four ordinary words.

CAPEE

DUCIL

WYSORD

YEMINT

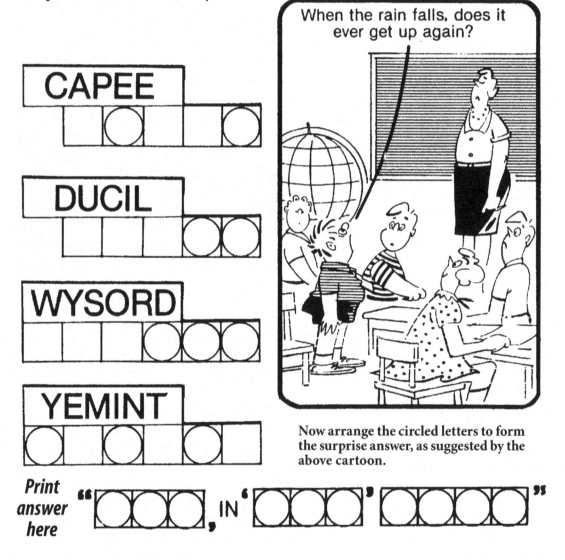

When the rain falls, does it ever get up again?

Now arrange the circled letters to form the surprise answer, as suggested by the above cartoon.

Print answer here “___, IN ‘____’ _____”

PUZZLE 63

JUMBLE®

Unscramble these four Jumbles, one letter to each square, to form four ordinary words.

NALAC

RADUG

TOWBES

DOOMIN

WHAT A PERSON MIGHT HAVE TO BE IN ORDER TO BLOW OUT ALL THOSE CANDLES ON HIS BIRTHDAY CAKE.

Now arrange the circled letters to form the surprise answer, as suggested by the above cartoon.

Print answer here ◯◯◯◯-◯◯◯◯◯◯

PUZZLE 64

JUMBLE®

Unscramble these four Jumbles, one letter to each square, to form four ordinary words.

BLEAC

SIGUE

LAISOC

KERROB

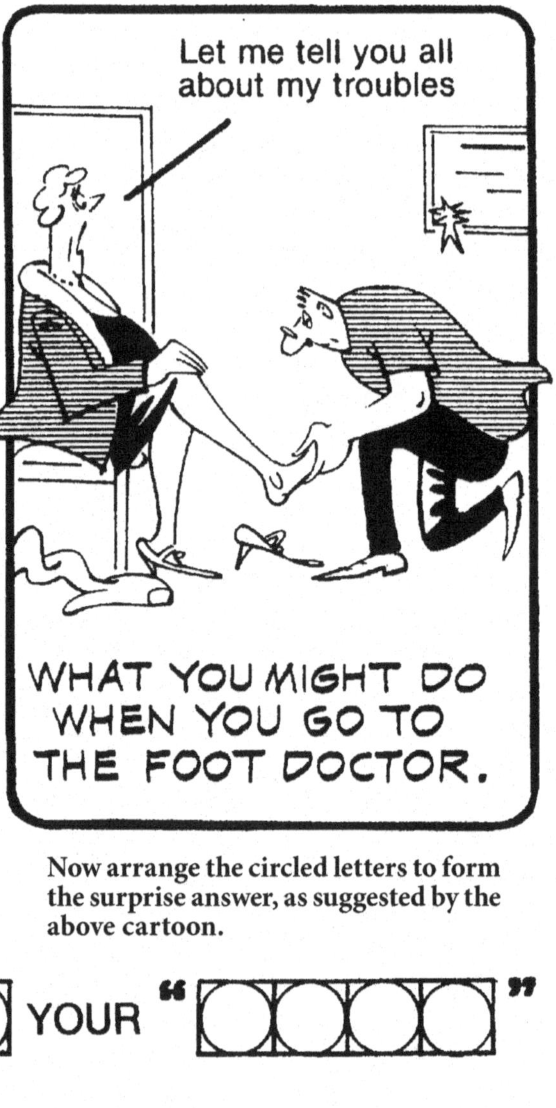
Let me tell you all about my troubles
WHAT YOU MIGHT DO WHEN YOU GO TO THE FOOT DOCTOR.

Now arrange the circled letters to form the surprise answer, as suggested by the above cartoon.

Print answer here ○○○○ YOUR "○○○○○"

PUZZLE 65

JUMBLE®

Unscramble these four Jumbles, one letter to each square, to form four ordinary words.

MERIN

ZYCAR

TELEEB

VUSSER

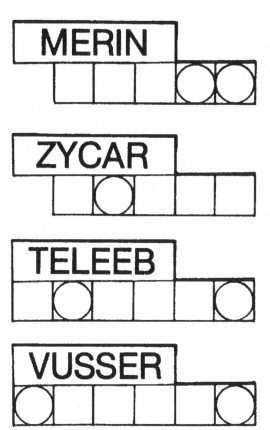

Better get some new accounts or you're in trouble
AJAX CO.

WHAT A PERSON MIGHT GO INTO UNLESS HE SHIFTS FOR HIMSELF.

Now arrange the circled letters to form the surprise answer, as suggested by the above cartoon.

Print answer here

PUZZLE 66

JUMBLE®

Unscramble these four Jumbles, one letter to each square, to form four ordinary words.

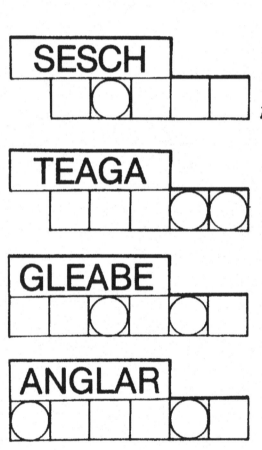

SESCH

TEAGA

GLEABE

ANGLAR

WHAT THE ACTION IN THAT SOAP OPERA WORKED ITSELF UP TO.

Now arrange the circled letters to form the surprise answer, as suggested by the above cartoon.

Print answer here

JUMBLE®

Unscramble these four Jumbles, one letter to each square, to form four ordinary words.

LECEX

PRUSN

DUCLOY

VOINEC

WHAT THE DELIVERY BOY FROM THE PIZZA PARLOR RODE.

Now arrange the circled letters to form the surprise answer, as suggested by the above cartoon.

Print answer here A " "

PUZZLE 68

JUMBLE®

Unscramble these four Jumbles, one letter to each square, to form four ordinary words.

SYTUL

KALOC

DACARE

ELDAHN

THE SERGEANT KNEW WHEN TO DO THIS.

Now arrange the circled letters to form the surprise answer, as suggested by the above cartoon.

Print answer here ◯◯◯◯ A ◯◯◯◯

PUZZLE 69

JUMBLE®

Unscramble these four Jumbles, one letter to each square, to form four ordinary words.

WOALG

LYRYD

MEEBOC

WYIHNN

WHAT THE QUEEN THREATENED TO DO WHEN THE KING CAME HOME LATE ONE NIGHT.

Now arrange the circled letters to form the surprise answer, as suggested by the above cartoon.

Print answer here " "

PUZZLE 70

JUMBLE®

Unscramble these four Jumbles, one letter to each square, to form four ordinary words.

REEMB

SUGES

TAGASH

INSEPP

Don't you think we should call the plumber, dear?
WHAT KIND OF SHOES WAS HE WEARING WHEN HE TACKLED THAT FLOODED BASEMENT?

Now arrange the circled letters to form the surprise answer, as suggested by the above cartoon.

Print answer here

PUZZLE 71

JUMBLE®

Unscramble these four Jumbles, one letter to each square, to form four ordinary words.

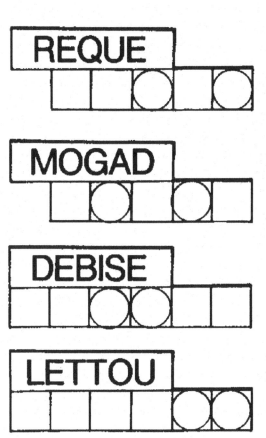

REQUE

MOGAD

DEBISE

LETTOU

Listen to what we did today
PEOPLE WITH TIRELESS ENERGY SOON BECOME THIS.

Now arrange the circled letters to form the surprise answer, as suggested by the above cartoon.

Print answer here

PUZZLE
72

JUMBLE®

Unscramble these four Jumbles, one letter to each square, to form four ordinary words.

URRJO

ROSYR

DRIZAW

IMCUPE

WHAT THEY HAD TO OPEN IN ORDER TO ENTER THE HAUNTED HOUSE.

Now arrange the circled letters to form the surprise answer, as suggested by the above cartoon.

Print answer here THE " "

JUMBLE®

Unscramble these four Jumbles, one letter to each square, to form four ordinary words.

IRRAB

NEVAK

SACCES

HURGOT

WHAT IT WAS
FOR THE PEEPING TOM
WHEN HE WAS CAUGHT
LOOKING THROUGH
AN OPEN WINDOW.

Now arrange the circled letters to form the surprise answer, as suggested by the above cartoon.

Print answer here

PUZZLE 74

JUMBLE®

Unscramble these four Jumbles, one letter to each square, to form four ordinary words.

LOTEX

ALLIV

WEGNIT

HALTEL

I've always believed a man should be the boss
WHAT IT SOMETIMES TAKES TO LAND A SPOUSE.

Now arrange the circled letters to form the surprise answer, as suggested by the above cartoon.

Print answer here A " "

JUMBLE®

Unscramble these four Jumbles, one letter to each square, to form four ordinary words.

VEEKO

YAWLB

TELTEK

ENICKS

Sounds like a prowler
MIGHT BE USE-FUL IF YOU WANT TO LEARN ABOUT THE "SHOCKING" SE-CRETS IN THAT CLOSET.

Now arrange the circled letters to form the surprise answer, as suggested by the above cartoon.

Print answer here A " "

PUZZLE 76

JUMBLE®

Unscramble these four Jumbles, one letter to each square, to form four ordinary words.

EEDUL

TYJET

SNUFIO

YUBILS

Makes you want to fall asleep on the spot
WHAT A PILLOW SALESMAN HAS TO BE A MASTER OF.

Now arrange the circled letters to form the surprise answer, as suggested by the above cartoon.

Print answer here THE

PUZZLE 77

JUMBLE®

Unscramble these four Jumbles, one letter to each square, to form four ordinary words.

OONES

CEROW

BEWOLB

STEACK

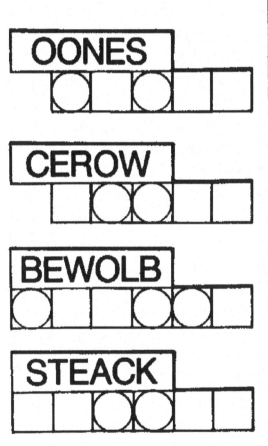

WHAT A NAME DROPPER IS APT TO DO.

Now arrange the circled letters to form the surprise answer, as suggested by the above cartoon.

Print answer here HIS " "

JUMBLE®

Unscramble these four Jumbles, one letter to each square, to form four ordinary words.

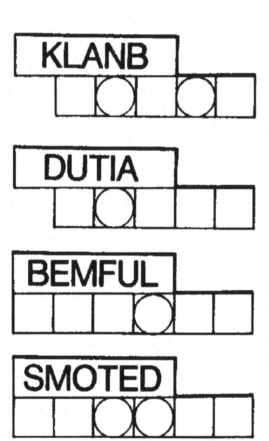

KLANB

DUTIA

BEMFUL

SMOTED

WHAT THE INVENTOR OF THE FIRST AUTO-MATIC PACKAGING MACHINE MADE.

Now arrange the circled letters to form the surprise answer, as suggested by the above cartoon.

Print answer here A

PUZZLE 79

JUMBLE®

Unscramble these four Jumbles, one letter to each square, to form four ordinary words.

WHART

BASAH

ZURBEZ

ALPECA

WHAT THOSE OLD-TIME RUSSIANS FOUGHT.

Now arrange the circled letters to form the surprise answer, as suggested by the above cartoon.

Print answer here " "

JUMBLE®

Unscramble these four Jumbles, one letter to each square, to form four ordinary words.

She's new
No telephone calls . . .
No loud records . . .
HE WON'T STAND FOR ANYTHING!

ATAGE

EFING

YONDOB

MOCNOM

Now arrange the circled letters to form the surprise answer, as suggested by the above cartoon.

Print answer here

PUZZLE 81

JUMBLE®

Unscramble these four Jumbles, one letter to each square, to form four ordinary words.

TILMI

ANBOT

PERUSH

ROTTET

Gulp!
WHAT THE SUGAR TYCOON GOT AS HE WAS TRYING TO PROPOSE MARRIAGE.

Now arrange the circled letters to form the surprise answer, as suggested by the above cartoon.

Print answer here A ◯◯◯◯ IN HIS ◯◯◯◯◯◯

PUZZLE 82

JUMBLE®

Unscramble these four Jumbles, one letter to each square, to form four ordinary words.

URIOC

DEFAM

GAMANE

LEPOAR

You've got it all, kid!

SOMETHING A LOT OF WOMEN ARE TAKEN IN BY.

Now arrange the circled letters to form the surprise answer, as suggested by the above cartoon.

Print answer here

PUZZLE 83

JUMBLE®

Unscramble these four Jumbles, one letter to each square, to form four ordinary words.

NYWEL

ASTEE

RALLOF

ENTAIN

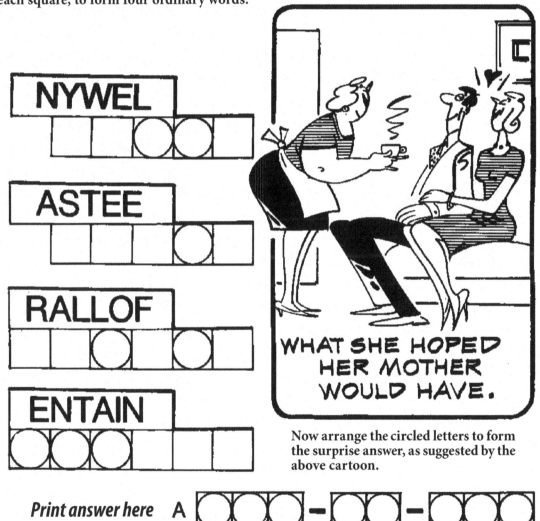

WHAT SHE HOPED HER MOTHER WOULD HAVE.

Now arrange the circled letters to form the surprise answer, as suggested by the above cartoon.

Print answer here A ___ - __ - ___

PUZZLE
84

JUMBLE®

Unscramble these four Jumbles, one letter to each square, to form four ordinary words.

KULCC

LAQUI

UMDAAR

KEENAW

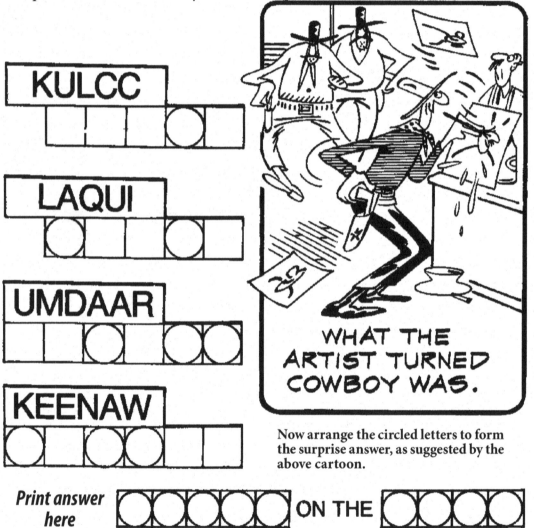

WHAT THE ARTIST TURNED COWBOY WAS.

Now arrange the circled letters to form the surprise answer, as suggested by the above cartoon.

Print answer here ON THE

PUZZLE 85

JUMBLE®

Unscramble these four Jumbles, one letter to each square, to form four ordinary words.

KLANE

PLYSH

RAVEEB

CLEMPO

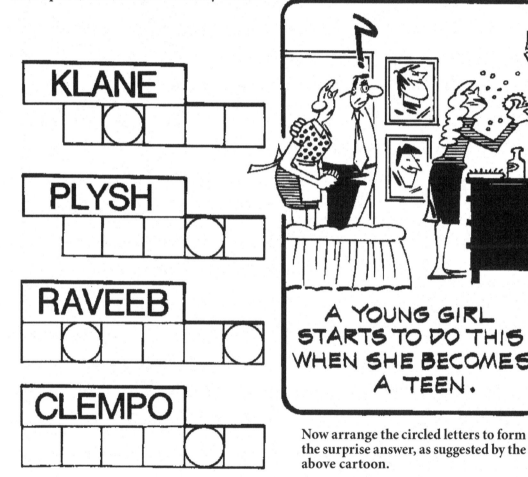

A YOUNG GIRL STARTS TO DO THIS WHEN SHE BECOMES A TEEN.

Now arrange the circled letters to form the surprise answer, as suggested by the above cartoon.

Print answer here

PUZZLE 86

JUMBLE®

Unscramble these four Jumbles, one letter to each square, to form four ordinary words.

ILVIC

FLAIN

TERVID

GUNJEL

HE WOULDN'T BE IN SUCH A HURRY IF HE KNEW HE WAS THIS.

Now arrange the circled letters to form the surprise answer, as suggested by the above cartoon.

Print answer here ○○○○○○○ TO ○○○○○

PUZZLE 87

JUMBLE®

Unscramble these four Jumbles, one letter to each square, to form four ordinary words.

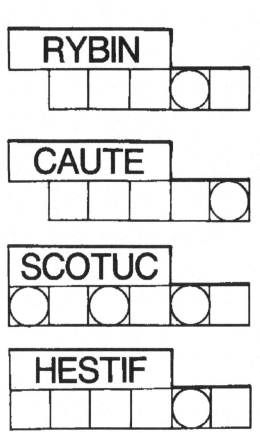

RYBIN

CAUTE

SCOTUC

HESTIF

WHEN HIS WIFE GAVE BIRTH TO QUINTUPLETS, HE COULD HARDLY BELIEVE THIS.

Now arrange the circled letters to form the surprise answer, as suggested by the above cartoon.

Print answer here HIS " "

Unscramble these four Jumbles, one letter to each square, to form four ordinary words.

DALGE

YEEND

RENITE

NADDIC

WHERE DO ZOMBIES
LIKE TO SIT
WHEN THEY GO TO
THE MOVIES?

Now arrange the circled letters to form the surprise answer, as suggested by the above cartoon.

Print answer here

JUMBLE®

Unscramble these four Jumbles, one letter to each square, to form four ordinary words.

UPTIL

ASTUE

TAPCER

OOLANG

Maybe I'm too tough on them
WHAT TEACHER SAID WHEN HE SAT ON A TACK.

Now arrange the circled letters to form the surprise answer, as suggested by the above cartoon.

Print answer here I ◯◯◯ THE ◯◯◯◯◯◯

JUMBLE®

Unscramble these four Jumbles, one letter to each square, to form four ordinary words.

YOGGS

ENTAK

CUSSEN

GORUBE

WHAT YOU'D EXPECT TO HAVE FOR BREAKFAST AT A LIGHTHOUSE.

Now arrange the circled letters to form the surprise answer, as suggested by the above cartoon.

Print answer here " " &

PUZZLE 91

JUMBLE®

Unscramble these four Jumbles, one letter to each square, to form four ordinary words.

CHUGO

TARAL

SLARIO

YESWIL

I hear it's terrific

WHAT YOU MIGHT SEE AT A PLANETARIUM.

Now arrange the circled letters to form the surprise answer, as suggested by the above cartoon.

Print answer here AN ◯◯◯-◯◯◯◯◯ ◯◯◯◯◯

PUZZLE 92

JUMBLE®

Unscramble these four Jumbles, one letter to each square, to form four ordinary words.

LOFOR

HOWSY

RANTIM

DORPAN

WHAT HE DID EVERY TIME HE BOUGHT A SUIT.

Now arrange the circled letters to form the surprise answer, as suggested by the above cartoon.

Print answer here

PUZZLE 93

JUMBLE®

Unscramble these four Jumbles, one letter to each square, to form four ordinary words.

NILOG

CUIJY

ENMECT

HONGIM

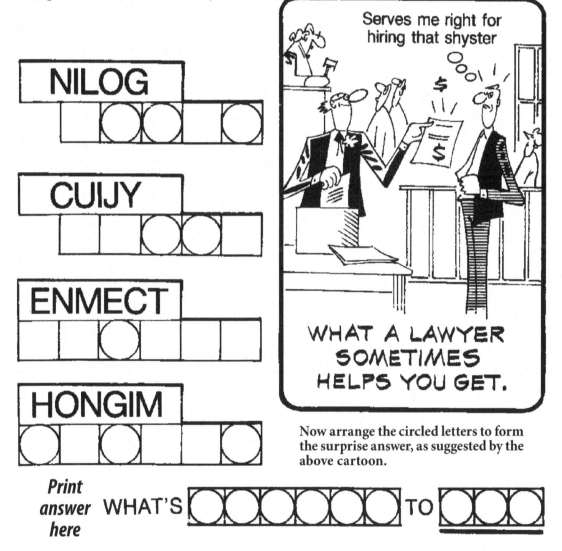

Serves me right for hiring that shyster
$
$
WHAT A LAWYER SOMETIMES HELPS YOU GET.

Now arrange the circled letters to form the surprise answer, as suggested by the above cartoon.

Print answer here WHAT'S ______ TO ___

PUZZLE 94

JUMBLE®

Unscramble these four Jumbles, one letter to each square, to form four ordinary words.

HUVOC

BANIC

ZEBRAL

THOOSE

Don't pay any attention to any of that
WHAT WAS ALL THAT TALK DOWN AT THE GARBAGE DUMP?

Now arrange the circled letters to form the surprise answer, as suggested by the above cartoon.

Print answer here A OF

PUZZLE 95

JUMBLE®

Unscramble these four Jumbles, one letter to each square, to form four ordinary words.

PALLE

LEREC

RORTER

TURBAP

WHAT THAT FIRST TAVERN IN THE ARCTIC WAS CALLED.

Now arrange the circled letters to form the surprise answer, as suggested by the above cartoon.

Print answer here THE

PUZZLE 96

JUMBLE®

Unscramble these four Jumbles, one letter to each square, to form four ordinary words.

RIFAR

DREEL

RITHEE

THELME

WHAT THAT STAG WAS FORCED TO RUN FOR.

Now arrange the circled letters to form the surprise answer, as suggested by the above cartoon.

Print answer here " "

PUZZLE 97

JUMBLE®

Unscramble these four Jumbles, one letter to each square, to form four ordinary words.

NAIPO

DIFOR

UNGOAT

RACCES

WHEN LOOKING FOR BARGAINS, YOU MIGHT GO THERE.

Now arrange the circled letters to form the surprise answer, as suggested by the above cartoon.

Print answer here WHERE THE “ ”

PUZZLE 98

JUMBLE®

Unscramble these four Jumbles, one letter to each square, to form four ordinary words.

LOOGI

PLOIT

SEVURS

PUNACK

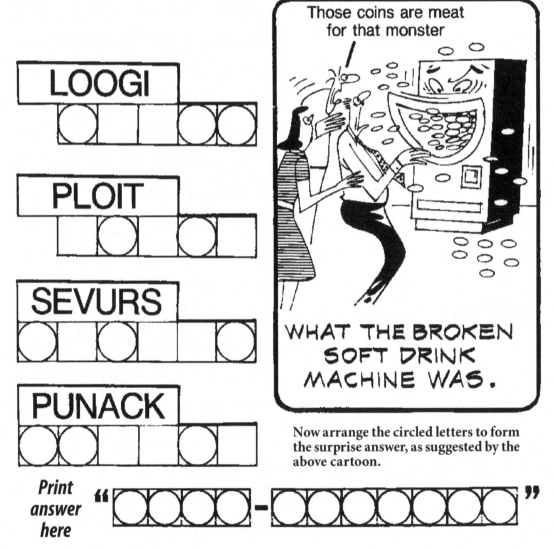

Those coins are meat for that monster
WHAT THE BROKEN SOFT DRINK MACHINE WAS.

Now arrange the circled letters to form the surprise answer, as suggested by the above cartoon.

Print answer here “____-_______”

PUZZLE 99

JUMBLE®

Unscramble these four Jumbles, one letter to each square, to form four ordinary words.

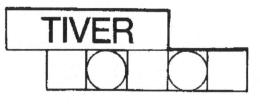

TIVER

WULAF

GRAUSY

CLISHE

I hope we're as smart as we think we are
WHAT GOOD CAMOUFLAGE IS.

Now arrange the circled letters to form the surprise answer, as suggested by the above cartoon.

Print answer here

Unscramble these four Jumbles, one letter to each square, to form four ordinary words.

RIQUE

ENSIO

CLEFEE

TERRAH

WHAT THAT GREAT HORROR FILM WAS.

Now arrange the circled letters to form the surprise answer, as suggested by the above cartoon.

Print answer here " ◯◯◯◯◯◯ – ◯◯◯◯ "

JUMBLE®

Unscramble these four Jumbles, one letter to each square, to form four ordinary words.

HOYNE

MERIC

GLEMIT

DROWBY

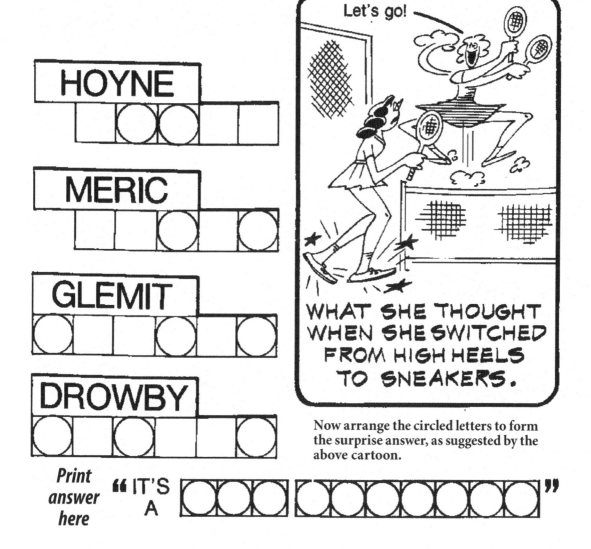

Let's go!
WHAT SHE THOUGHT WHEN SHE SWITCHED FROM HIGH HEELS TO SNEAKERS.

Now arrange the circled letters to form the surprise answer, as suggested by the above cartoon.

Print answer here "IT'S A ___ ________"

PUZZLE 102

JUMBLE®

Unscramble these four Jumbles, one letter to each square, to form four ordinary words.

BELZA

ORFYT

KLINTE

CURPSE

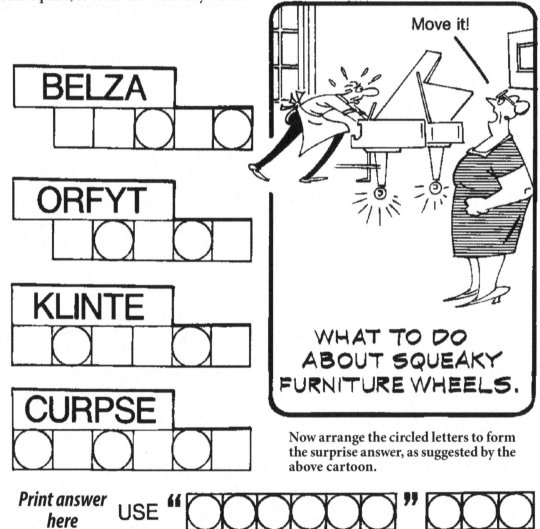

Move it!
WHAT TO DO ABOUT SQUEAKY FURNITURE WHEELS.

Now arrange the circled letters to form the surprise answer, as suggested by the above cartoon.

Print answer here USE " "

PUZZLE 103

JUMBLE®

Unscramble these four Jumbles, one letter to each square, to form four ordinary words.

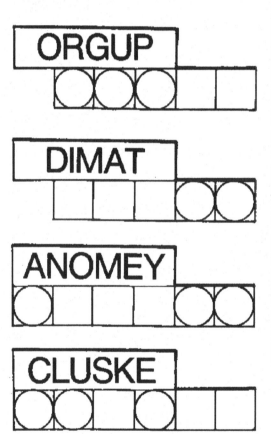

ORGUP

DIMAT

ANOMEY

CLUSKE

YAK YAK YAK YAK

A TIRESOME PERSON ALWAYS TAKES HIS TIME DOING THIS.

Now arrange the circled letters to form the surprise answer, as suggested by the above cartoon.

Print answer here

PUZZLE 104

JUMBLE®

Unscramble these four Jumbles, one letter to each square, to form four ordinary words.

NOYGA

TANEC

KLUBEC

INYELC

WHAT HER COMPANIONS CALLED THAT STUPID HEN.

Now arrange the circled letters to form the surprise answer, as suggested by the above cartoon.

Print answer here A

JUMBLE®

Unscramble these four Jumbles, one letter to each square, to form four ordinary words.

CHOPE

GATEA

AMMAND

LAGYAX

WHAT THE VICTIM THOUGHT WHEN THE ROBBER STUFFED HIS MOUTH WITH A DIRTY CLOTH.

Now arrange the circled letters to form the surprise answer, as suggested by the above cartoon.

Print answer here "THAT'S ◯◯ ◯◯◯ ◯◯◯"

PUZZLE 106

JUMBLE®

Unscramble these four Jumbles, one letter to each square, to form four ordinary words.

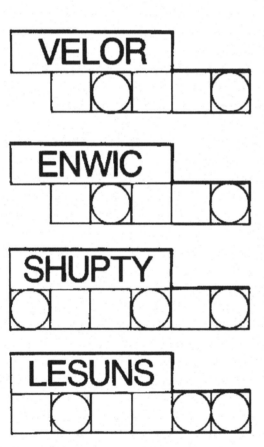

VELOR

ENWIC

SHUPTY

LESUNS

A SCANDALMONGER IS MOST HAPPY WHEN SHE CONFESSES THIS.

Now arrange the circled letters to form the surprise answer, as suggested by the above cartoon.

Print answer here THE ◯◯◯◯ OF ◯◯◯◯◯◯

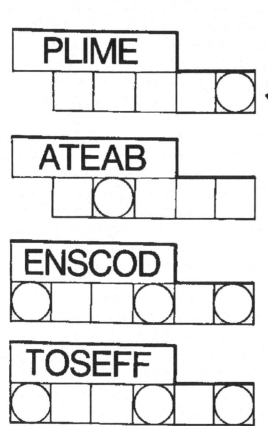

JUMBLE®

Unscramble these four Jumbles, one letter to each square, to form four ordinary words.

PLIME

ATEAB

ENSCOD

TOSEFF

JOKES ARE ALWAYS IMPROVED WHEN THEY'RE THIS.

Now arrange the circled letters to form the surprise answer, as suggested by the above cartoon.

Print answer here BY THE

JUMBLE®

Unscramble these four Jumbles, one letter to each square, to form four ordinary words.

ACTEX

MAFLE

COAMIS

WHARRO

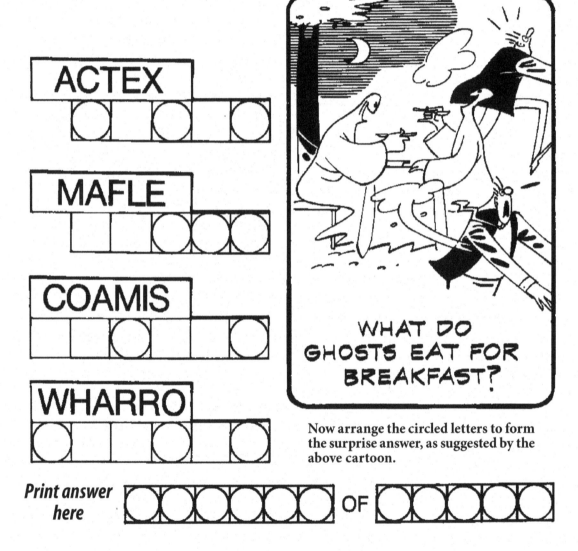

WHAT DO GHOSTS EAT FOR BREAKFAST?

Now arrange the circled letters to form the surprise answer, as suggested by the above cartoon.

Print answer here OF

JUMBLE®

Unscramble these four Jumbles, one letter to each square, to form four ordinary words.

KNACS

DEHIC

CLAYKE

FRAMOT

Here! Take skunk—
it's just as good

WHAT SHE CALLED HIM WHEN HE WELSHED ON HIS PROMISE TO BUY HER A NEW MINK.

Now arrange the circled letters to form the surprise answer, as suggested by the above cartoon.

Print answer here

PUZZLE 110

JUMBLE®

Unscramble these four Jumbles, one letter to each square, to form four ordinary words.

BROIN

PEELO

MYCLAB

ORSOUP

SEEMS TO GROW ABUNDANTLY IN THIS YARD.

Now arrange the circled letters to form the surprise answer, as suggested by the above cartoon.

Print answer here A

PUZZLE
111

JUMBLE®

Unscramble these four Jumbles, one letter to each square, to form four ordinary words.

SWEYN

DRUGO

TYBLUS

DILFED

WHAT THE YOUNG COUPLE CALLED THEIR DRIVE TO LOVERS LANE.

Now arrange the circled letters to form the surprise answer, as suggested by the above cartoon.

Print answer here A " "

Unscramble these four Jumbles, one letter to each square, to form four ordinary words.

ROWCE

EYAPE

TALNED

DOAFER

She's the best

SHE BECAME THE
CHIEF ARTIST
BECAUSE SHE
WAS ----

Now arrange the circled letters to form the surprise answer, as suggested by the above cartoon.

Print answer here ◯◯◯ " ◯◯◯◯◯ – ◯◯ "

PUZZLE 113

JUMBLE®

Unscramble these four Jumbles, one letter to each square, to form four ordinary words.

SMIPK

TEAGA

SNEFTA

DRIMBO

Give me more speed
HOW THE YACHT RACE LEFT THE NERVOUS SKIPPER.

Now arrange the circled letters to form the surprise answer, as suggested by the above cartoon.

Print answer here ◯◯◯◯ UP IN ◯◯◯◯◯

JUMBLE®

Unscramble these four Jumbles, one letter to each square, to form four ordinary words.

IMPER

THRAW

TINISS

GOMURE

UNFAIR
WE NEED A RAISE
NO MORE

WHAT THE ANGRY FIELD HANDS CALLED THEIR GRIEVANCES.

Now arrange the circled letters to form the surprise answer, as suggested by the above cartoon.

Print answer here ________ OF ______

PUZZLE 115

JUMBLE®

Unscramble these four Jumbles, one letter to each square, to form four ordinary words.

SMACH

SUROE

STELEN

RYSLIG

You weren't watching
Neither were you
WHAT CARELESS-NESS SOMETIMES LEADS TO.

Now arrange the circled letters to form the surprise answer, as suggested by the above cartoon.

Print answer here

JUMBLE®

Unscramble these four Jumbles, one letter to each square, to form four ordinary words.

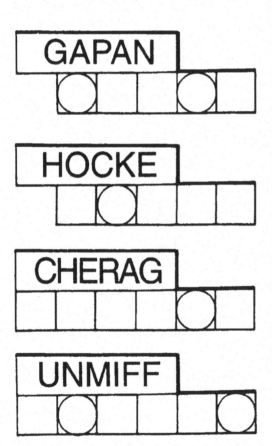

GAPAN

HOCKE

CHERAG

UNMIFF

Not again?
I just felt the urge
WHY SHE KEPT CHANGING HER WALLPAPER.

Now arrange the circled letters to form the surprise answer, as suggested by the above cartoon.

Print answer here IT WAS A ____-__

PUZZLE 117

JUMBLE®

Unscramble these four Jumbles, one letter to each square, to form four ordinary words.

GREEM

WALBY

MYSALE

RALLUP

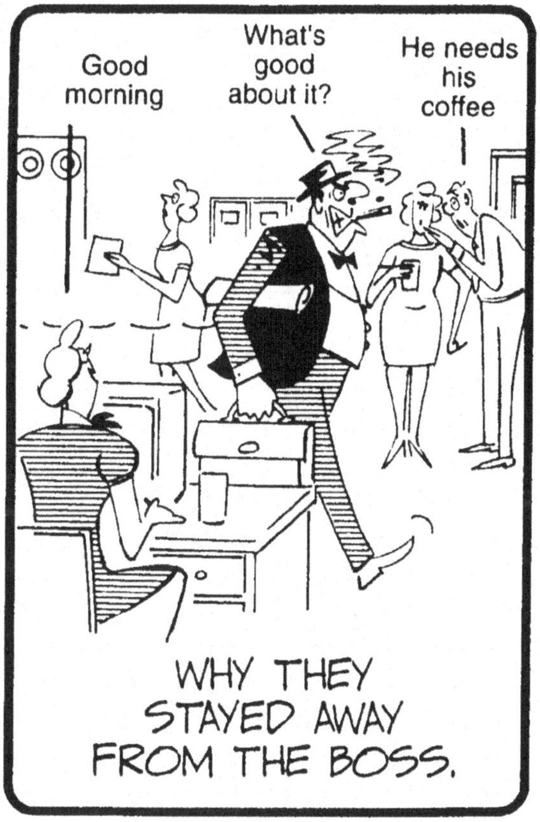
Good morning
What's good about it?
He needs his coffee
WHY THEY STAYED AWAY FROM THE BOSS.

Now arrange the circled letters to form the surprise answer, as suggested by the above cartoon.

Print answer here HE WAS

PUZZLE 118

JUMBLE®

Unscramble these four Jumbles, one letter to each square, to form four ordinary words.

FLOYT

BELLI

BANCOR

CUSCOT

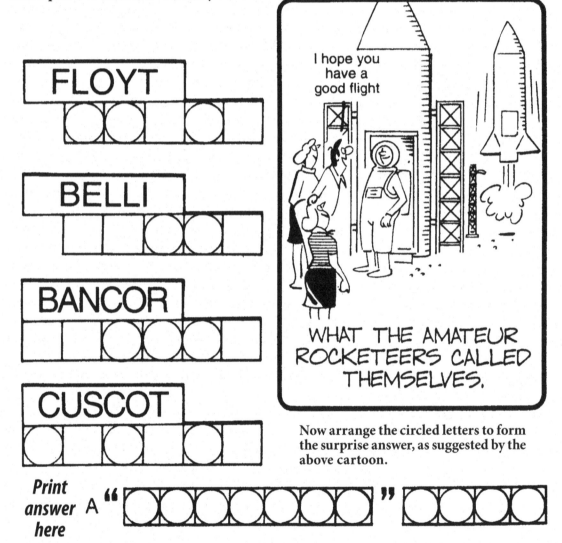

I hope you have a good flight

WHAT THE AMATEUR ROCKETEERS CALLED THEMSELVES.

Now arrange the circled letters to form the surprise answer, as suggested by the above cartoon.

Print answer here A “ ”

PUZZLE 119

JUMBLE®

Unscramble these four Jumbles, one letter to each square, to form four ordinary words.

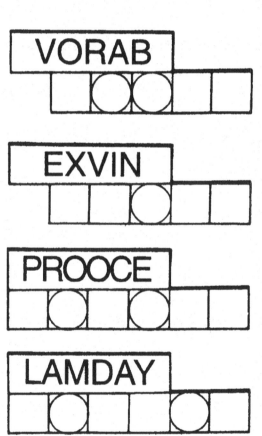

VORAB

EXVIN

PROOCE

LAMDAY

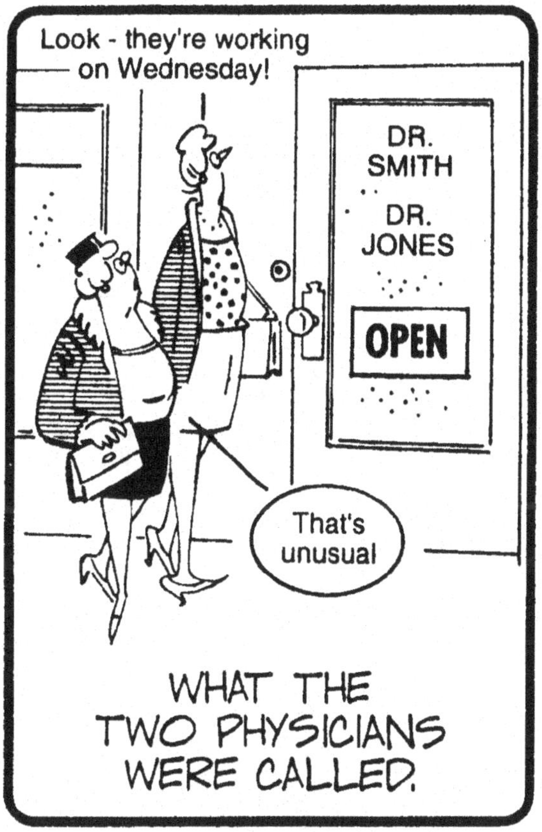
Look - they're working on Wednesday!
DR. SMITH
DR. JONES
OPEN
That's unusual

WHAT THE TWO PHYSICIANS WERE CALLED.

Now arrange the circled letters to form the surprise answer, as suggested by the above cartoon.

Print answer here A “ ”

JUMBLE®

Unscramble these four Jumbles, one letter to each square, to form four ordinary words.

MARRE

DORAH

INDOWS

TUGONI

You're getting all dirty
WHAT WERE THE LITTLE COWPOKES DOING AT THE CORRAL?

Now arrange the circled letters to form the surprise answer, as suggested by the above cartoon.

Print answer here THEY WERE ______' ______

PUZZLE 121

JUMBLE®

Unscramble these four Jumbles, one letter to each square, to form four ordinary words.

DRYIT

TINJO

LETEBE

ANSOOL

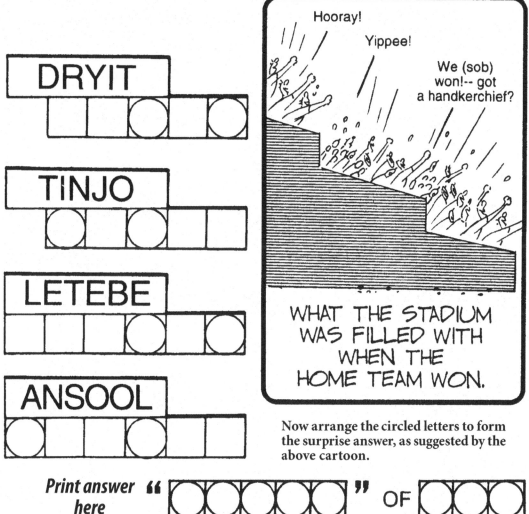

Hooray!
Yippee!
We (sob) won!-- got a handkerchief?

WHAT THE STADIUM WAS FILLED WITH WHEN THE HOME TEAM WON.

Now arrange the circled letters to form the surprise answer, as suggested by the above cartoon.

Print answer here " ◯◯◯◯◯ " OF ◯◯◯

PUZZLE 122

JUMBLE®

Unscramble these four Jumbles, one letter to each square, to form four ordinary words.

TAIRE

WOYLL

NAKTIE

CAUABS

I don't believe this bad streak
WHAT THE LOSING GAMBLER DID.

Now arrange the circled letters to form the surprise answer, as suggested by the above cartoon.

Print answer here HIS

PUZZLE 123

JUMBLE®

Unscramble these four Jumbles, one letter to each square, to form four ordinary words.

LULET

ALAFT

FREEHI

QUAPEL

You eat more than you pick
WHAT THE APPLE PICKER THOUGHT HIS JOB WAS.

Now arrange the circled letters to form the surprise answer, as suggested by the above cartoon.

Print answer here " - "

PUZZLE 124

JUMBLE®

Unscramble these four Jumbles, one letter to each square, to form four ordinary words.

GLONI

KINDE

BROJEB

GUYSAR

WHAT THE CORRUPT BANKER DID FOR THE CIRCUS.

Now arrange the circled letters to form the surprise answer, as suggested by the above cartoon.

Print answer here HE ________ THE ______

PUZZLE 125

JUMBLE®

Unscramble these four Jumbles, one letter to each square, to form four ordinary words.

SOSBA

PAUNC

TOTIPE

SURSED

I quit-- it's too hard
Me, too

WHAT THE SPACE SCHOOL DROPOUTS CALLED THEMSELVES.

Now arrange the circled letters to form the surprise answer, as suggested by the above cartoon.

Print answer here " ______ - _____ "

PUZZLE 126

JUMBLE®

Unscramble these four Jumbles, one letter to each square, to form four ordinary words.

GRAWE

PUGOR

PEKAUM

CORNAY

WHAT A PULP MILL MANAGER NEVER RUNS OUT OF.

Now arrange the circled letters to form the surprise answer, as suggested by the above cartoon.

Print answer here

PUZZLE 127

JUMBLE®

Unscramble these four Jumbles, one letter to each square, to form four ordinary words.

CENAP

TOAQU

CUROGH

SMEECH

WHAT YOU MIGHT CALL THE DIRECTOR OF THE WESTERN PLAY.

Now arrange the circled letters to form the surprise answer, as suggested by the above cartoon.

Print answer here A

PUZZLE 128

JUMBLE®

Unscramble these four Jumbles, one letter to each square, to form four ordinary words.

SINOE

CEENF

COPHON

TENSOX

He says YOU can go right in
MAYOR

IT'S HELPFUL TO HAVE THIS WHEN YOU WANT SOMETHING AT CITY HALL.

Now arrange the circled letters to form the surprise answer, as suggested by the above cartoon.

Print answer here

PUZZLE 129

JUMBLE®

Unscramble these four Jumbles, one letter to each square, to form four ordinary words.

NAWTY

GIRRO

WYIHNN

GREENE

It still works
WHEN THE ALARM CLOCK FELL IN THE WATER IT WAS ---

Now arrange the circled letters to form the surprise answer, as suggested by the above cartoon.

Print answer here “ ”

JUMBLE®

Unscramble these four Jumbles, one letter to each square, to form four ordinary words.

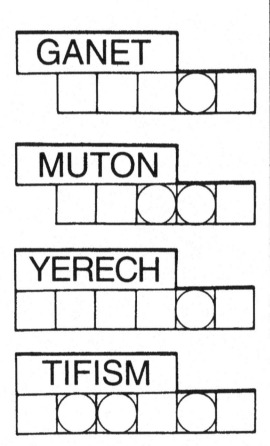

GANET

MUTON

YERECH

TIFISM

You're fired!
HOW UNSUCCESSFUL ARCHEOLOGISTS OFTEN FIND THEIR CAREERS.

Now arrange the circled letters to form the surprise answer, as suggested by the above cartoon.

Print answer here ◯◯ "◯◯◯◯◯"

PUZZLE 131

JUMBLE®

Unscramble these four Jumbles, one letter to each square, to form four ordinary words.

GWIRN

CIKYP

AQUOPE

STOUMT

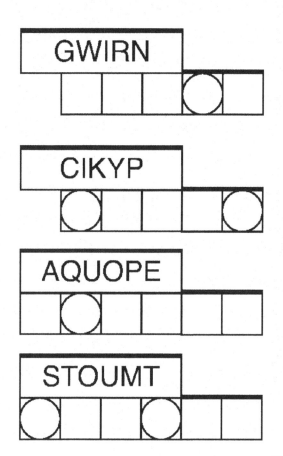

Oh, Daddy! I love him so much! He and Flicka will be best friends.
You get your checkbook. I'll get the paperwork.
IF HE WAS GOING TO BUY ANOTHER HORSE, HE WOULD HAVE TO ---

Now arrange the circled letters to form the surprise answer, as suggested by the above cartoon.

Print answer here

PUZZLE 132

JUMBLE®

Unscramble these four Jumbles, one letter to each square, to form four ordinary words.

SIHOT

ENPOR

CANLEG

DARIHO

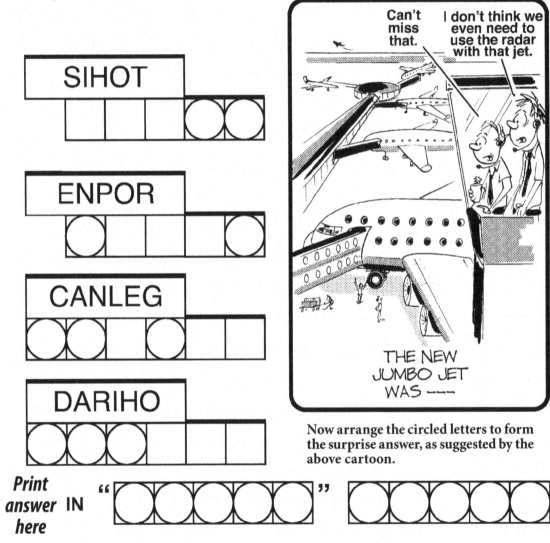

Can't miss that.
I don't think we even need to use the radar with that jet.
THE NEW JUMBO JET WAS ---

Now arrange the circled letters to form the surprise answer, as suggested by the above cartoon.

Print answer here IN " ◯◯◯◯◯ " ◯◯◯◯◯

PUZZLE 133

JUMBLE®

Unscramble these four Jumbles, one letter to each square, to form four ordinary words.

ANFIT

DAGEL

ESSMEA

OXTERV

Coach, how could you lose 105 to 3?
If you haven't played this game, I don't want to hear it from you!
WHEN HE ANSWERED QUESTIONS ABOUT ALL THE TOUCHDOWNS SCORED AGAINST HIS TEAM, HE ---

Now arrange the circled letters to form the surprise answer, as suggested by the above cartoon.

Print answer here

PUZZLE 134

JUMBLE®

Unscramble these four Jumbles, one letter to each square, to form four ordinary words.

KURYM

GIREM

MECYDO

TENSCH

How could I forget to change out your brain chip? Now I have to reset everything.

THE TECHNICIAN FORGOT TO CHANGE THE ANDROID'S POSITRONIC BRAIN. HE NEEDED A ---

Now arrange the circled letters to form the surprise answer, as suggested by the above cartoon.

Print answer here “ ◯◯ - ◯◯◯◯◯ - ◯◯ ”

PUZZLE 135

JUMBLE®

Unscramble these four Jumbles, one letter to each square, to form four ordinary words.

WARLC

ONDUM

PEERRF

POMSIE

Great round! I wouldn't play anywhere else.
I agree. Let's just have fish and chips today.
CONCESSIONS
AFTER FINISHING THE 18TH HOLE, THEY STOPPED TO EAT A ---

Now arrange the circled letters to form the surprise answer, as suggested by the above cartoon.

Print answer here ___ - ______ _____

JUMBLE®

Unscramble these four Jumbles, one letter to each square, to form four ordinary words.

LASIA

VONLE

DRYLAH

VABHEE

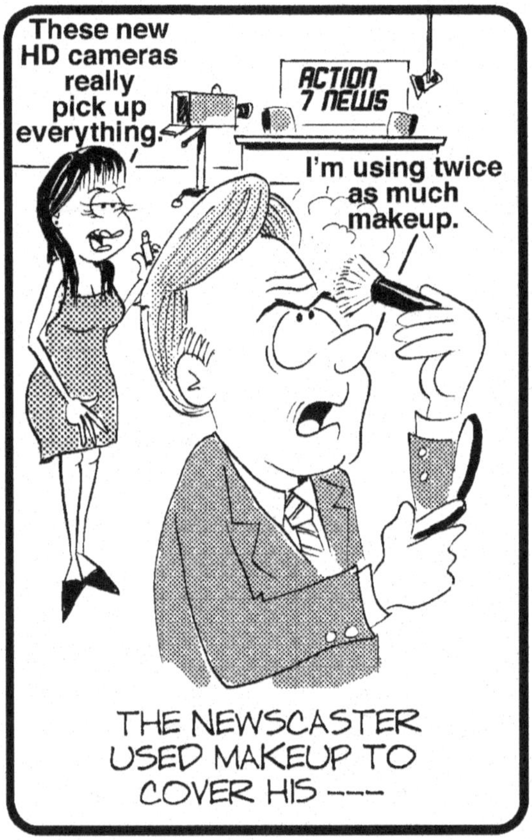
These new HD cameras really pick up everything.
ACTION 7 NEWS
I'm using twice as much makeup.
THE NEWSCASTER USED MAKEUP TO COVER HIS ---

Now arrange the circled letters to form the surprise answer, as suggested by the above cartoon.

Print answer here

PUZZLE 137

JUMBLE®

Unscramble these four Jumbles, one letter to each square, to form four ordinary words.

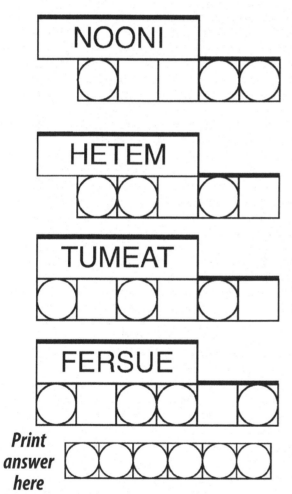

NOONI

HETEM

TUMEAT

FERSUE

I'm telling you, Tracy, I wasn't there!
Well, the lie detector says otherwise.
THE POLYGRAPH TEST WAS THE ---

Now arrange the circled letters to form the surprise answer, as suggested by the above cartoon.

Print answer here

PUZZLE 138

JUMBLE®

Unscramble these four Jumbles, one letter to each square, to form four ordinary words.

CRAHN

DORPU

WULLAF

ULOTTE

Are we good to go?
The judge just signed it.
THE POLICE SEARCHED THE BUILDING BECAUSE IT WAS ---

Now arrange the circled letters to form the surprise answer, as suggested by the above cartoon.

Print answer here

PUZZLE
139

JUMBLE®

Unscramble these four Jumbles, one letter to each square, to form four ordinary words.

WARBL

THACC

LOGPAL

SKYCIT

I always wanted to run away with the circus.
Awesome!
DRACULA ENJOYED GOING TO THE TRANSYLVANIA CIRCUS TO WATCH THE ---

Now arrange the circled letters to form the surprise answer, as suggested by the above cartoon.

Print answer here " ◯◯◯◯-◯◯◯◯ "

JUMBLE®

Unscramble these four Jumbles, one letter to each square, to form four ordinary words.

KCIRB

HUGAL

TANVIE

RETBAY

You have to move farther away. Your smoke is coming right into the building.
We can't help which way the wind is blowing.
THE NON-SMOKERS MET WITH THE SMOKERS TO ---

Now arrange the circled letters to form the surprise answer, as suggested by the above cartoon.

Print answer here

PUZZLE 141

JUMBLE®

Unscramble these four Jumbles, one letter to each square, to form four ordinary words.

RIFUT

HISSU

REDGED

PIXREE

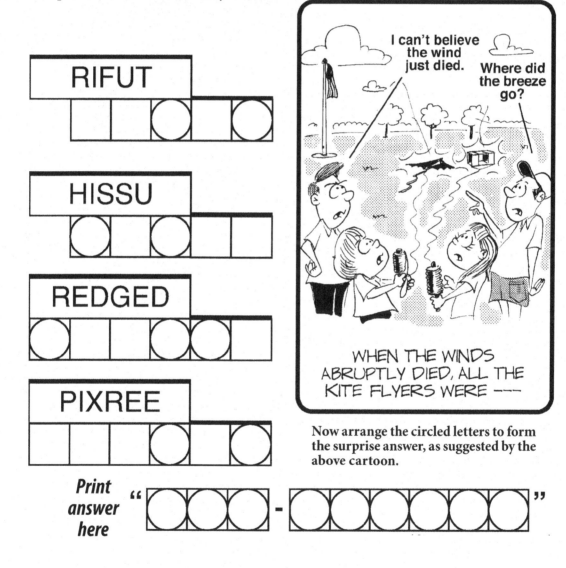

I can't believe the wind just died.
Where did the breeze go?
WHEN THE WINDS ABRUPTLY DIED, ALL THE KITE FLYERS WERE ---

Now arrange the circled letters to form the surprise answer, as suggested by the above cartoon.

Print answer here " - "

PUZZLE 142

JUMBLE®

Unscramble these four Jumbles, one letter to each square, to form four ordinary words.

DERNT

HOVSE

SOREIR

FLUBIA

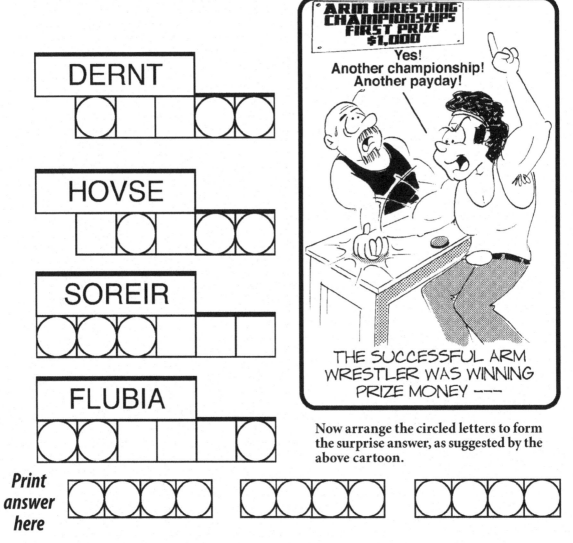

ARM WRESTLING CHAMPIONSHIPS FIRST PRIZE $1,000
Yes! Another championship! Another payday!
THE SUCCESSFUL ARM WRESTLER WAS WINNING PRIZE MONEY ---

Now arrange the circled letters to form the surprise answer, as suggested by the above cartoon.

Print answer here

JUMBLE®

Unscramble these four Jumbles, one letter to each square, to form four ordinary words.

VEALV

CETEL

CLEEEF

SAACUB

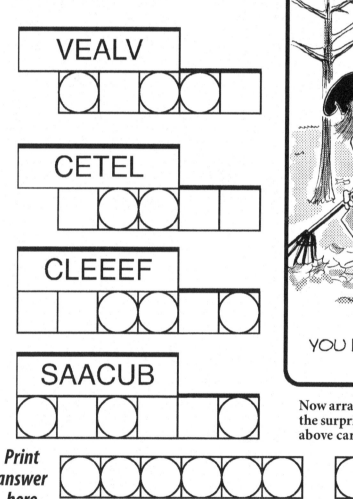

What are you waiting for?
There are a few that haven't fallen yet.

YOU KNOW IT'S AUTUMN WHEN THE ---

Now arrange the circled letters to form the surprise answer, as suggested by the above cartoon.

Print answer here

PUZZLE 144

JUMBLE®

Unscramble these four Jumbles, one letter to each square, to form four ordinary words.

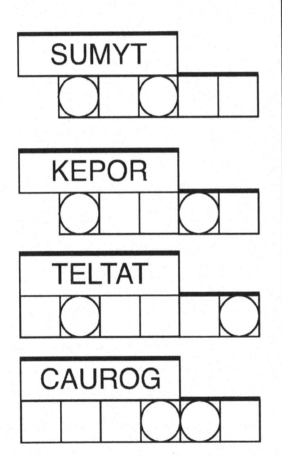

SUMYT

KEPOR

TELTAT

CAUROG

Let's just order lunch poolside.
That sounds like a great idea to me, honey.
THE VACATIONING BOOK LOVERS WERE ON THE ---

Now arrange the circled letters to form the surprise answer, as suggested by the above cartoon.

Print answer here

PUZZLE 145

JUMBLE®

Unscramble these four Jumbles, one letter to each square, to form four ordinary words.

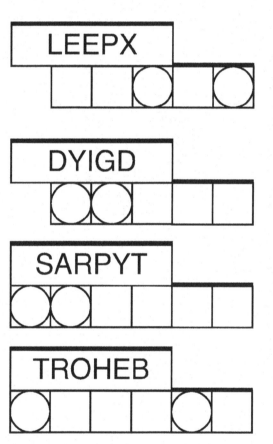

LEEPX

DYIGD

SARPYT

TROHEB

Do you have anything larger?
KING KONG WENT TO THE NEW YORK CITY FRUIT STAND IN SEARCH OF A ---

Now arrange the circled letters to form the surprise answer, as suggested by the above cartoon.

Print answer here

PUZZLE 146

JUMBLE®

Unscramble these four Jumbles, one letter to each square, to form four ordinary words.

NUROD

BUGRY

CHOSOM

HERTOB

Now arrange the circled letters to form the surprise answer, as suggested by the above cartoon.

Print answer here

PUZZLE 147

JUMBLE®

Unscramble these four Jumbles, one letter to each square, to form four ordinary words.

SALFH

DENEY

TOERAT

RABNER

THE SELECTION OF NEW GLASSES WAS RIGHT ---

Now arrange the circled letters to form the surprise answer, as suggested by the above cartoon.

Print answer here HER

PUZZLE 148

JUMBLE®

Unscramble these four Jumbles, one letter to each square, to form four ordinary words.

GADEA

DIFUL

TANEUP

JEBTOC

AFTER THE HORSE'S GIRLFRIEND BROKE UP WITH HIM, HE HAD A ---

Now arrange the circled letters to form the surprise answer, as suggested by the above cartoon.

Print answer here

PUZZLE 149

JUMBLE®

Unscramble these four Jumbles, one letter to each square, to form four ordinary words.

LUWAF

CANET

BEGOIL

RASPIN

Studios from $200 a month. FREE A/C! Great Views!
HE HAD TROUBLE FINDING TENANTS FOR HIS DEATH VALLEY APARTMENTS, EVEN WITH THEIR ---

Now arrange the circled letters to form the surprise answer, as suggested by the above cartoon.

Print answer here

PUZZLE 150

JUMBLE®

Unscramble these four Jumbles, one letter to each square, to form four ordinary words.

NOONI

HITTG

CASAUB

LIPCEV

EVERYTHING MUST GO!
Here are all the jeans.
We need to make some room for our new stock.
These are great bargains.
80% OFF!
LAST YEAR'S STYLE
Buy 1 Get 1 Free!

TO GET RID OF LAST SEASON'S FASHIONS, THE BOUTIQUE HAD THIS TYPE OF SALE.

Now arrange the circled letters to form the surprise answer, as suggested by the above cartoon.

Print answer here A "○○○○○○○-○○○"

PUZZLE 151

JUMBLE®

Unscramble these four Jumbles, one letter to each square, to form four ordinary words.

GIMER

LOGIO

RUYHAR

RAKTEA

Ed, you come from a long line of barbers. It's your turn to take over.
Thanks, Dad.
STECKLEY & SONS

THE BARBERSHOP HAD BEEN IN HIS FAMILY FOR YEARS AND IT WAS HIS TURN TO RUN IT . . . IT WAS HIS ---

Now arrange the circled letters to form the surprise answer, as suggested by the above cartoon.

Print answer here " ____ - ______ "

JUMBLE®

Unscramble these four Jumbles, one letter to each square, to form four ordinary words.

KULFE

AOIDU

BOLEGB

DISBEE

Read this and it will take you from collecting tickets to finding patron's seats.
EXIT
Follow Me

THE USHER AT THE THEATER WANTED TO BE AN AUTHOR, SO HE WROTE A ---

Now arrange the circled letters to form the surprise answer, as suggested by the above cartoon.

Print answer here

PUZZLE 153

JUMBLE®

Unscramble these four Jumbles, one letter to each square, to form four ordinary words.

ADDEF

NARGD

SELUUF

MELTHE

I said sell!
NYSE
New York Shrubs Express
He's made a killing on selling stocks short.
So, now he's investing in bushes?
NYSE
HE WAS ABLE TO AFFORD HIS NEW LANDSCAPING AFTER MAKING SO MUCH MONEY IN HIS ---

Now arrange the circled letters to form the surprise answer, as suggested by the above cartoon.

Print answer here

JUMBLE®

Unscramble these four Jumbles, one letter to each square, to form four ordinary words.

CIRPE

KILYM

WARIYA

REELVC

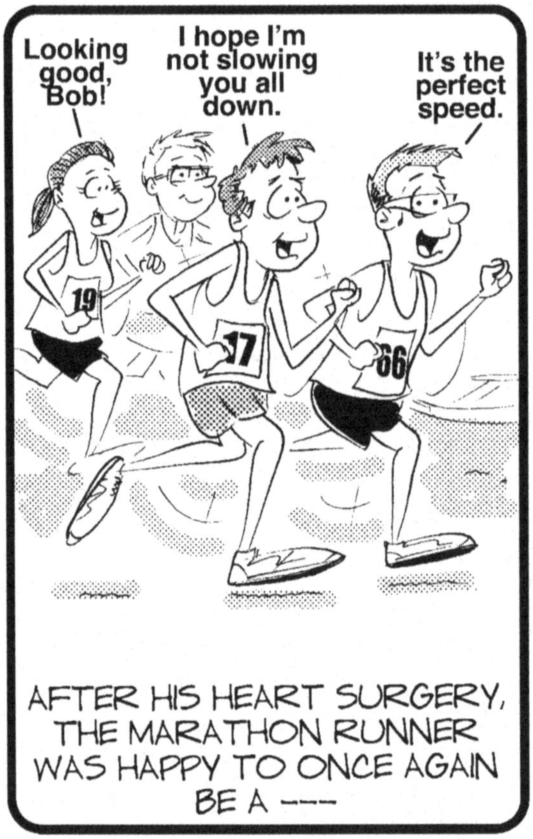
Looking good, Bob!
I hope I'm not slowing you all down.
It's the perfect speed.
19
17
66
AFTER HIS HEART SURGERY, THE MARATHON RUNNER WAS HAPPY TO ONCE AGAIN BE A ---

Now arrange the circled letters to form the surprise answer, as suggested by the above cartoon.

Print answer here -

PUZZLE 155

JUMBLE®

Unscramble these four Jumbles, one letter to each square, to form four ordinary words.

TUCOL

YALPP

HBIRDY

CUNEBO

What! Who took my eggs?
THERE WERE NO EGGS IN THE HENHOUSE BECAUSE THEY HAD BEEN ---

Now arrange the circled letters to form the surprise answer, as suggested by the above cartoon.

Print answer here

PUZZLE 156

JUMBLE®

Unscramble these four Jumbles, one letter to each square, to form four ordinary words.

TRIYD

DUMIH

NILDAN

FUBTEF

How about kicking the ball, Cam?
I wish he'd pull the weeds in our yard.
Ha! Mine's chasing butterflies.
WHILE WATCHING THEIR KIDS PLAY SOCCER, THE PARENTS HAD A ---

Now arrange the circled letters to form the surprise answer, as suggested by the above cartoon.

Print answer here

JUMBLE®

Unscramble these four Jumbles, one letter to each square, to form four ordinary words.

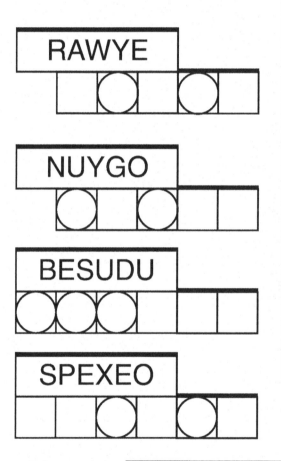

RAWYE

NUYGO

BESUDU

SPEXEO

You're my hero! How can I thank you?
I'd love to talk, but I have a lot more people to help today.
DAILY PLANET
WHEN HE WASN'T WORKING AS A MILD-MANNERED REPORTER, CLARK KENT WAS ---

Now arrange the circled letters to form the surprise answer, as suggested by the above cartoon.

Print answer here

PUZZLE
158

JUMBLE®

Unscramble these four Jumbles, one letter to each square, to form four ordinary words.

ONTEK

ODUES

GRYTEN

DARTIE

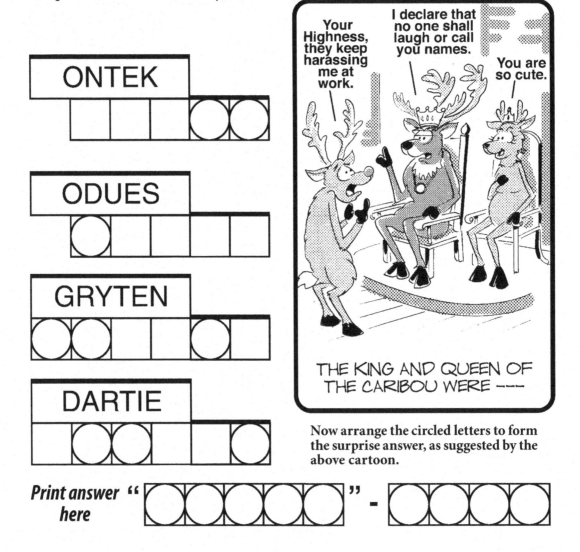

Your Highness, they keep harassing me at work.
I declare that no one shall laugh or call you names.
You are so cute.
THE KING AND QUEEN OF THE CARIBOU WERE ---

Now arrange the circled letters to form the surprise answer, as suggested by the above cartoon.

Print answer here " " -

PUZZLE 159

JUMBLE®

Unscramble these four Jumbles, one letter to each square, to form four ordinary words.

PONAR

RABOV

CELLOA

ZYGTIL

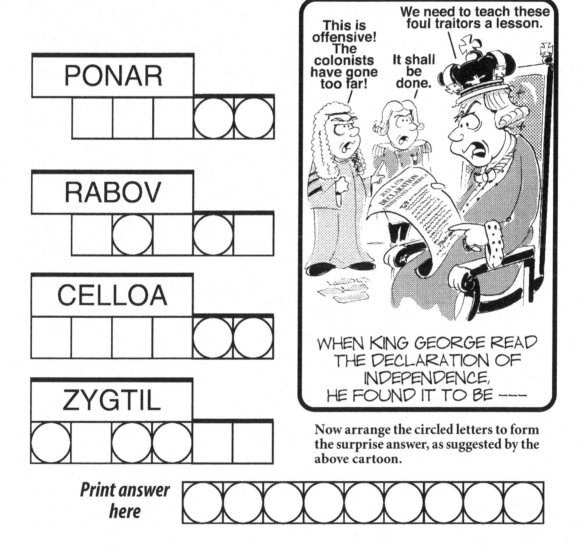

This is offensive! The colonists have gone too far!
It shall be done.
We need to teach these foul traitors a lesson.
DECLARATION
WHEN KING GEORGE READ THE DECLARATION OF INDEPENDENCE, HE FOUND IT TO BE ---

Now arrange the circled letters to form the surprise answer, as suggested by the above cartoon.

Print answer here

PUZZLE 160

JUMBLE®

Unscramble these four Jumbles, one letter to each square, to form four ordinary words.

HAALP

FNORT

RIVDET

DUNSED

Have you been watching Bruce Willis movies all night?
Yes, it's the John McClane-a-thon! He's so awesome! I pity anyone who stands in his way.
SHE ADORED BRUCE WILLIS AND ALWAYS WOULD, BECAUSE SHE WAS A ---

Now arrange the circled letters to form the surprise answer, as suggested by the above cartoon.

Print answer here

Touchdown JUMBLE®

CHALLENGER

PUZZLES

PUZZLE 161

JUMBLE®

Unscramble these six Jumbles, one letter to each square, to form six ordinary words.

SNIYKN

SPOXEE

LEANIF

TACNAV

SATJUD

THURCC

WELCOME TO BEHEMOTH BANK
RECEIVE .02% ON A SAVINGS ACCOUNT .04% ON A CHECKING ACCOUNT
Open an account today and get a free toaster!
THE BANK'S GRAND OPENING SUFFERED FROM ---

Now arrange the circled letters to form the surprise answer, as suggested by the above cartoon.

Print answer here

PUZZLE 162

JUMBLE®

Unscramble these six Jumbles, one letter to each square, to form six ordinary words.

SWARLP

RATDOW

AMARUT

DINGIO

PURNGS

ANEEGG

Be careful, guys. It's vital that we get that in the new building undamaged.
THE CHURCH'S RELOCATION REQUIRED ---

Now arrange the circled letters to form the surprise answer, as suggested by the above cartoon.

Print answer here

AN

PUZZLE 163

JUMBLE®

Unscramble these six Jumbles, one letter to each square, to form six ordinary words.

FREESU

YELVLA

TIQUAC

DEHDUL

SARBOB

PANKUC

I can't believe he wins every time.
Well, when you don't look for a job, you have a lot of time to stretch.
THE LIMBO CHAMPION WAS ONE.

Now arrange the circled letters to form the surprise answer, as suggested by the above cartoon.

Print answer here

AN

PUZZLE 164

JUMBLE®

Unscramble these six Jumbles, one letter to each square, to form six ordinary words.

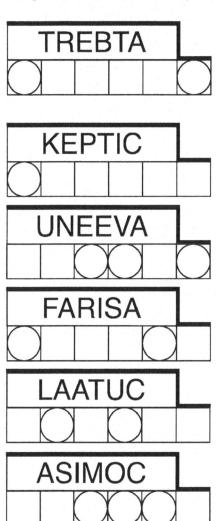

TREBTA

KEPTIC

UNEEVA

FARISA

LAATUC

ASIMOC

Is this supposed to be out?
Miss, why won't my window open?
Can I move?
Where's my drink?

THE FLIGHT ATTENDANT WAS STARTING TO FEEL THE ---

Now arrange the circled letters to form the surprise answer, as suggested by the above cartoon.

Print answer here

JUMBLE®

Unscramble these six Jumbles, one letter to each square, to form six ordinary words.

NITHEZ

GLONOB

MASHAT

SARSUE

CXDEEE

TIRREW

Do you remember going to Boblo Island as a kid? I loved taking the boat to get there.
Oh, yeah! My family would go every year. Do you remember...
HUNTING ON A WINDY DAY ALLOWED THEM TO ---

Now arrange the circled letters to form the surprise answer, as suggested by the above cartoon.

Print answer here

PUZZLE 166

JUMBLE®

Unscramble these six Jumbles, one letter to each square, to form six ordinary words.

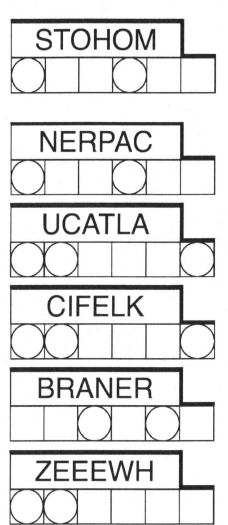

STOHOM

NERPAC

UCATLA

CIFELK

BRANER

ZEEEWH

I think we should name him after my father, King Charles.

WHAT THEY WOULD END UP CALLING THE HUMPBACK KING AND QUEEN'S SON.

Now arrange the circled letters to form the surprise answer, as suggested by the above cartoon.

Print answer here

THE ______ __ "________"

PUZZLE 167

JUMBLE®

Unscramble these six Jumbles, one letter to each square, to form six ordinary words.

WAQUKS

FUMNIF

DGUTEB

SNITIS

QUTAEE

IGLGEG

How many times do I have to ask you to take out the trash?
Will you lay off! I'll get to it right after my show.
THE TICK
WHEN THE BEETLE'S WIFE ASKED HIM TO TAKE OUT THE GARBAGE FOR THE THIRD TIME, HE SAID THIS.

Now arrange the circled letters to form the surprise answer, as suggested by the above cartoon.

Print answer here

PUZZLE 168

JUMBLE®

Unscramble these six Jumbles, one letter to each square, to form six ordinary words.

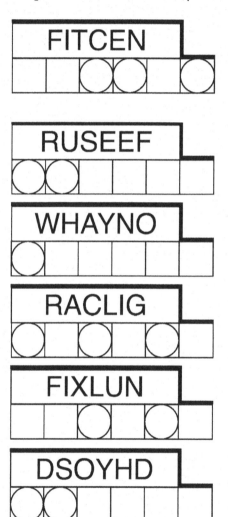

FITCEN

RUSEEF

WHAYNO

RACLIG

FIXLUN

DSOYHD

How many dads are here today?
I'm not sure. I'll count. 1, 2, 3, 4...
I've got five grand-babies.
That's a lot.
#1 Dad
WHEN THEY COUNTED THE NUMBER OF DADS AT THE COOKOUT, THEY ENDED UP WITH ---

Now arrange the circled letters to form the surprise answer, as suggested by the above cartoon.

Print answer here

JUMBLE®

Unscramble these six Jumbles, one letter to each square, to form six ordinary words.

CENTIJ

CERNDH

TRYOWH

TAMENH

AWENOP

CEESXS

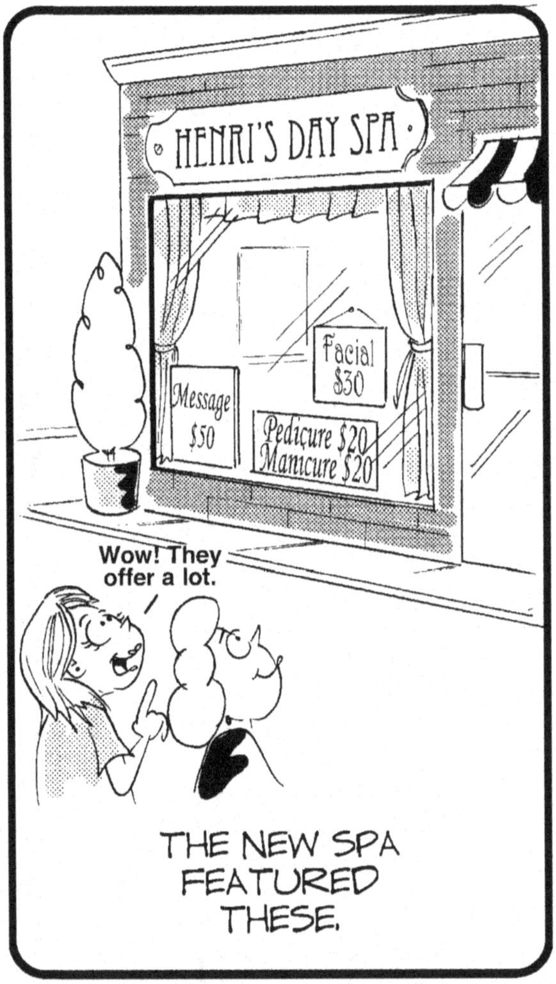
HENRI'S DAY SPA
Facial $30
Message $50
Pedicure $20
Manicure $20
Wow! They offer a lot.
THE NEW SPA FEATURED THESE.

Now arrange the circled letters to form the surprise answer, as suggested by the above cartoon.

Print answer here

PUZZLE 170

JUMBLE®

Unscramble these six Jumbles, one letter to each square, to form six ordinary words.

YSSLOG

CEANGY

DOURNG

TINTNE

KOEYCJ

SAGINS

Wow! When did we get all these?
They've been coming all month.
Holidays Happy
HO HO HO
Christmas Merry
JUMBLE

YOU GET SO MANY CARDS DURING THE HOLIDAYS BECAUSE IT'S ---

Now arrange the circled letters to form the surprise answer, as suggested by the above cartoon.

Print answer here

PUZZLE 171

JUMBLE®

Unscramble these six Jumbles, one letter to each square, to form six ordinary words.

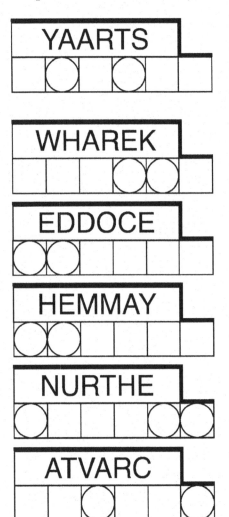

YAARTS

WHAREK

EDDOCE

HEMMAY

NURTHE

ATVARC

This is awful! Can't you get anything right?
NICK

COLD EGGS AND LUKEWARM COFFEE CAN RESULT IN ---

Now arrange the circled letters to form the surprise answer, as suggested by the above cartoon.

Print answer here

"○○○○○○" ○○○○○○○

PUZZLE 172

JUMBLE®

Unscramble these six Jumbles, one letter to each square, to form six ordinary words.

CUNNEA

FUTTIO

RAJUAG

DITNIC

SPICHY

ROOBLE

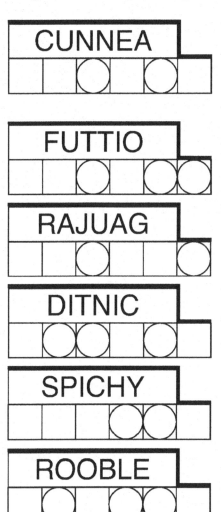

...and ACTION!
WHAT THE ACTOR NEEDED FOR THE FISHING SCENE.

Now arrange the circled letters to form the surprise answer, as suggested by the above cartoon.

Print answer here

A " ◯◯◯◯◯◯◯ " ◯◯◯◯◯◯◯◯

PUZZLE 173

JUMBLE®

Unscramble these six Jumbles, one letter to each square, to form six ordinary words.

ERASHE

GLERCY

CAMIOT

GLEANB

GRINTY

YURLOH

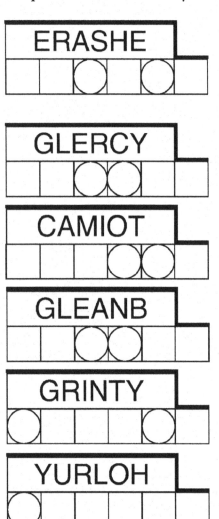

Pay up or we'll go after your income
WHEN THE PARSLEY FARMER DIDN'T PAY HIS DEBT, HE FACED ---

Now arrange the circled letters to form the surprise answer, as suggested by the above cartoon.

Print answer here

" - "

PUZZLE 174

JUMBLE®

Unscramble these six Jumbles, one letter to each square, to form six ordinary words.

DAPCIL

SNIULF

TINTEK

FATSIE

DEEBIS

SACULE

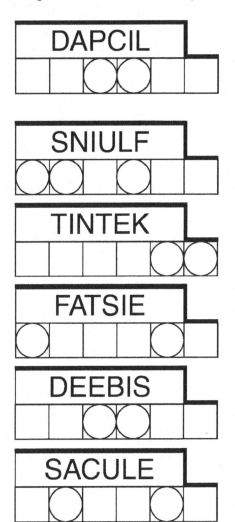

Our cash flow is down.
We need more members
WHAT THE EXERCISE CLUB LOST WHEN BUSINESS SLUMPED.

Now arrange the circled letters to form the surprise answer, as suggested by the above cartoon.

Print answer here

PUZZLE 175

JUMBLE®

Unscramble these six Jumbles, one letter to each square, to form six ordinary words.

GRONTS

ELLBOW

INSPOO

FAIRAS

DOGOLY

INGUMP

Nice work, Josh
Here's the latest, Sir
JOSH
JUMBLE

WHEN THE BOSS STOPPED BY, THE HARD-WORKING PRINTER MADE A ---

Now arrange the circled letters to form the surprise answer, as suggested by the above cartoon.

Print answer here

“ ”

PUZZLE 176

JUMBLE®

Unscramble these six Jumbles, one letter to each square, to form six ordinary words.

TAGASH

MYCALL

SNULES

TALFOA

HARTER

NOMCOM

Class, say good morning to Mr. Smith
404
Good morning, sir.

OFTEN FOUND IN "THE CLASSROOM"

Now arrange the circled letters to form the surprise answer, as suggested by the above cartoon.

Print answer here

PUZZLE 177

JUMBLE®

Unscramble these six Jumbles, one letter to each square, to form six ordinary words.

AMMBLE

ENGLET

TOUGUD

MABGIT

JERIGG

TICNID

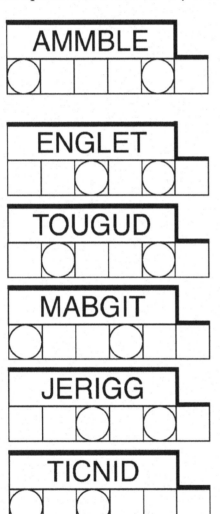

He's eating it all
He's got a big stomach to fill

WHY HE DECIDED TO EAT THE WHOLE PIE.

Now arrange the circled letters to form the surprise answer, as suggested by the above cartoon.

Print answer here

TO ◯◯◯◯◯◯◯ THE ◯◯◯◯◯

JUMBLE®

Unscramble these six Jumbles, one letter to each square, to form six ordinary words.

MERUDE

TOUTLE

HIRSLE

THECCI

ZURQAT

TRAYPI

I need some gas money
WHAT HE DID WHEN HE GAVE MOM A BIG HUG.

Now arrange the circled letters to form the surprise answer, as suggested by the above cartoon.

Print answer here

◯◯◯ THE "◯◯◯◯◯◯◯" ON ◯◯◯

PUZZLE 179

JUMBLE®

Unscramble these six Jumbles, one letter to each square, to form six ordinary words.

ROOLIE

SOUTID

PHILSO

WHYTOR

REESHA

GROUME

I'm down to my last chips

WEARING A TIE TO A FANCY CASINO DOESN'T MEAN YOU WON'T DO THIS.

Now arrange the circled letters to form the surprise answer, as suggested by the above cartoon.

Print answer here

PUZZLE 180

JUMBLE®

Unscramble these six Jumbles, one letter to each square, to form six ordinary words.

MODDEO

TYNTOK

GUNSLY

DISTOL

FLAUWL

GLIJEN

THEIR EXTENDED GOOD-BYE TURNED INTO A ---

Now arrange the circled letters to form the surprise answer, as suggested by the above cartoon.

Print answer here

" - "

Answers

1. **Jumbles:** CHAOS MANLY WEEVIL REFUGE
Answer: What some so-called "good buys" in Wall Street often turn out to be—"FAREWELLS"
2. **Jumbles:** EXACT WEDGE FROZEN VANITY
Answer: "What tennis!"—"FIVE X TWO"
3. **Jumbles:** GUILD ARRAY INJURY PARDON
Answer: What he called those people who acquitted him—A "GRAND" JURY
4. **Jumbles:** CLOAK DAUNT HIATUS BLOODY
Answer: How you sometimes end up if you go all out—ALL IN
5. **Jumbles:** SOAPY CHAFE TURGID POLITE
Answer: What were the prospects of departure during the big blizzard?—UP IN THE AIR
6. **Jumbles:** HAZEL ABOUT GIBBON BESIDE
Answer: The wheel was considered man's greatest invention until he got this—BEHIND IT
7. **Jumbles:** CROON ABYSS MODIFY NOODLE
Answer: How spring often arrives—"SODDEN-LY"
8. **Jumbles:** ACUTE OUNCE CONVEX TREMOR
Answer: What his favorite drink was—THE NEXT ONE
9. **Jumbles:** HEDGE CHASM JETSAM GIGOLO
Answer: The birthday cake had so many candles on it so he could make this—LIGHT OF HIS AGE
10. **Jumbles:** KNIFE CLOTH PILLAR LADING
Answer: What there was a lot of at the employment agency—"IDLE" TALK
11. **Jumbles:** SWOOP ENJOY POUNCE EQUITY
Answer: What a young man often has to do after deciding to pop the question—QUESTION THE POP
12. **Jumbles:** TOPAZ CYCLE MOROSE TRUANT
Answer: What the losing team was when there was an upset in the ballgame—UPSET
13. **Jumbles:** TEMPO SHEEP THEORY BOTTLE
Answer: What all those suggestions about improving the doughnut business seemed to have—HOLES IN THEM
14. **Jumbles:** AZURE BERET WALRUS ORIGIN
Answer: Some people might rise higher if they'd learn to do this—RISE EARLIER
15. **Jumbles:** FOCUS BALKY TORRID LEEWAY
Answer: What a hyphen permits you to do—BREAK YOUR WORD
16. **Jumbles:** CABIN LITHE GOSPEL HELPER
Answer: One isn't sure to say it—PERHAPS
17. **Jumbles:** COLIC FIORD BROKEN HAMPER
Answer: What a man who can't bear children undoubtedly is—NORMAL
18. **Jumbles:** GROOM FLOUT VISION HANDLE
Answer: What he was doing time for—"DOING" OTHERS
19. **Jumbles:** GUEST FROZE TURBAN NOVICE
Answer: A man with horse sense should know enough not to do this—BET ON ONE
20. **Jumbles:** BLIMP MAUVE HOPPER SUBMIT
Answer: What those twins were as alike as—"TOU-PEES" (two peas)
21. **Jumbles:** BOUGH FLUTE NOGGIN UPWARD
Answer: How the astronaut's wife was always happy to see him—"DOWN & OUT"
22. **Jumbles:** LURID PHONY PEWTER FORGER
Answer: What that little floor covering was—A "THROW" RUG
23. **Jumbles:** NAVAL JINGO BEYOND DEAFEN
Answer: People who are always flying into a rage sometimes end up making this—A BAD LANDING
24. **Jumbles:** DAISY FLAME CRAVAT MEASLY
Answer: What a practical joker does—AIMS TO TEASE
25. **Jumbles:** GULLY AIDED MOSQUE OUTING
Answer: How the old curmudgeon stalked out of that restaurant—IN A DUDGEON
26. **Jumbles:** CANAL BAKED SADIST CHROME
Answer: What they call some of those men who run the gaming tables—"DECK" HANDS
27. **Jumbles:** LOOSE ELDER PERMIT TONGUE
Answer: What an inhibited person usually is—TIED UP IN "NOTS"
28. **Jumbles:** MOOSE UNIFY TRIPLE ROTATE
Answer: What some speakers do when given the floor—RAISE THE ROOF
29. **Jumbles:** CROWN STAID GIBLET MALTED
Answer: A middle-age spread is simply this—A WAIST OF TIME
30. **Jumbles:** ABBEY WRATH LACKEY FAUCET
Answer: What the halfback was in his classroom work—WAY BACK
31. **Jumbles:** PARCH BEFIT JOYOUS DRUDGE
Answer: When it comes to love, an engagement ring is usually just this—A "BUY" PRODUCT
32. **Jumbles:** THINK AWOKE FORCED HOMAGE
Answer: Some guys don't know when to stop until they're told this—WHERE TO GO
33. **Jumbles:** DOGMA POACH FELLOW BANTER
Answer: What a yawn often is—A HOLE MADE BY A BORE
34. **Jumbles:** WHILE ABIDE TACKLE OVERDO
Answer: What the blacksmith did to his incompetent apprentice—BELLOWED AT HIM
35. **Jumbles:** VIPER QUOTA MUSKET CUDGEL
Answer: Medicine men are seldom what they're this—"QUACKED" UP TO BE
36. **Jumbles:** ELUDE JERKY FALTER ELIXIR
Answer: What the Scotsman who returned home late one night almost got—"KILT"
37. **Jumbles:** AISLE BUSHY FLAUNT PICKET
Answer: Those cars never run as smoothly as this—HE TALKS
38. **Jumbles:** HITCH ACRID ERMINE JURIST
Answer: What the violinist was up to—HIS CHIN IN MUSIC
39. **Jumbles:** TWEAK JOKER TURTLE DAMPEN
Answer: What a bureaucrat is—A RED TAPE WORM
40. **Jumbles:** JUMPY APRON RENDER MADMAN
Answer: What the golf addict's children called their father—"PAR-PAR"
41. **Jumbles:** DUSKY VITAL GOLFER LIQUID
Answer: Why he never got tired of proposing marriage to the moonshiner—HE LOVED HER STILL
42. **Jumbles:** BATHE POKER QUORUM STUCCO
Answer: What a duck hunter might be—A "QUACK" SHOT
43. **Jumbles:** BILGE FINAL PUSHER INHALE
Answer: He stoops low because he's anxious to do this—RISE HIGH
44. **Jumbles:** LINER ALIAS LAWFUL SOOTHE
Answer: What jokes told by mountain folk often are—"HILL-ARIOUS"
45. **Jumbles:** TRIPE BAGGY LAWYER BISHOP
Answer: What today's hangover might be connected with—THE WRATH OF GRAPES
46. **Jumbles:** EXILE AGENT STOLID PERSON
Answer: What she was, after a hard day's shopping—TIRED & "SPENT"

47. **Jumbles:** LIMIT FLUID GENTRY TOWARD
Answer: What a person who calls a spade a spade is probably about to give someone—A DIRTY "DIG"

48. **Jumbles:** CEASE FAITH SPRUCE TAUGHT
Answer: What's the best thing for nail-biting?—SHARP TEETH

49. **Jumbles:** ALTAR DRAMA CANINE IMPEDE
Answer: What getting rid of her maiden name was—HER MAIDEN AIM

50. **Jumbles:** ANNUL MACAW REFUGE TARGET
Answer: What's the best looking figure in geometry?—"A-CUTE" ANGLE

51. **Jumbles:** PAYEE SCARY NIMBLE ORCHID
Answer: What that aristocratic British pig was—THE "LARD" OF THE MANOR

52. **Jumbles:** SKULL BRAVO WEDGED LAYMAN
Answer: What bowling was—RIGHT DOWN HIS ALLEY

53. **Jumbles:** ANNOY OCCUR IMPAIR TREMOR
Answer: What wedding fees usually amount to—THE "UNION" RATE

54. **Jumbles:** KNIFE ABHOR COMMON EMPIRE
Answer: What the peaceful vegetarian was never about to do with anyone—PICK A BONE

55. **Jumbles:** ADMIT BRAIN GUZZLE PRIMER
Answer: The joke told by the tramp turned out to be this—A "BUMMER"

56. **Jumbles:** STOIC FUZZY MIDWAY GARBLE
Answer: What a man with a "burning" ambition is not apt to get—"FIRED"

57. **Jumbles:** BELIE DUCAT BRANCH GENTLE
Answer: How some people learn to drive a car—BY ACCIDENT

58. **Jumbles:** FORTY CHALK DECODE PATTER
Answer: What that well-to-do man was—HARD TO "DO"

59. **Jumbles:** ENTRY FAULT DEAFEN SUBMIT
Answer: How he seemed to be going to school—"ABSENTLY"

60. **Jumbles:** PURGE LAUGH EQUATE UTMOST
Answer: What that successful criminal was—A SMUG THUG

61. **Jumbles:** LEECH HAREM PLURAL SAFARI
Answer: A kleptomaniac "helps himself" because he can't do this—HELP HIMSELF

62. **Jumbles:** PEACE LUCID DROWSY ENMITY
Answer: "When the rain falls, does it ever get up again?"—"YES, IN 'DEW' TIME"

63. **Jumbles:** CANAL GUARD BESTOW DOMINO
Answer: What a person might have to be in order to blow out all those candles on his birthday cake—LONG-WINDED

64. **Jumbles:** CABLE GUISE SOCIAL BROKER
Answer: What you might do when you go to the foot doctor—BARE YOUR "SOLE"

65. **Jumbles:** MINER CRAZY BEETLE VERSUS
Answer: What a person might go into unless he shifts for himself—REVERSE

66. **Jumbles:** CHESS AGATE BEAGLE RAGLAN
Answer: What the action in that soap opera worked itself up to—A LATHER

67. **Jumbles:** EXCEL SPURN CLOUDY NOVICE
Answer: What the delivery boy from the pizza parlor rode—A "PIE" CYCLE

68. **Jumbles:** LUSTY CLOAK ARCADE HANDLE
Answer: The sergeant knew when to do this—CALL A HALT

69. **Jumbles:** AGLOW DRYLY BECOME WHINNY
Answer: What the queen threatened to do when the king came home late one night—"CROWN" HIM

70. **Jumbles:** EMBER GUESS AGHAST PEPSIN
Answer: What kind of shoes was he wearing when he tackled that flooded basement?—PUMPS

71. **Jumbles:** QUEER DOGMA BESIDE OUTLET
Answer: People with tireless energy soon become this—TIRESOME

72. **Jumbles:** JUROR SORRY WIZARD PUMICE
Answer: What they had to open in order to enter the haunted house—THE "SCREAM" DOOR

73. **Jumbles:** BRIAR KNAVE ACCESS TROUGH
Answer: What it was for the Peeping Tom when he was caught looking through an open window—CURTAINS

74. **Jumbles:** EXTOL VILLA TWINGE LETHAL
Answer: What it sometimes takes to land a spouse—A LITTLE "WILE"

75. **Jumbles:** EVOKE BYLAW KETTLE SICKEN
Answer: Might be useful if you want to learn about the "shocking" secrets in that closet—A "SKELETON" KEY

76. **Jumbles:** ELUDE JETTY FUSION BUSILY
Answer: What a pillow salesman has to be a master of—THE SOFT SELL

77. **Jumbles:** NOOSE COWER WOBBLE CASKET
Answer: What a name dropper is apt to do—BLOW HIS "KNOWS"

78. **Jumbles:** BLANK AUDIT FUMBLE MODEST
Answer: What the inventor of the first automatic packaging machine made—A BUNDLE

79. **Jumbles:** WRATH ABASH BUZZER PALACE
Answer: What those old-time Russians fought—"CZAR" WARS

80. **Jumbles:** AGATE FEIGN NOBODY COMMON
Answer: He won't stand for anything!—AN INFANT

81. **Jumbles:** LIMIT BATON PUSHER TOTTER
Answer: What the sugar tycoon got as he was trying to propose marriage—A LUMP IN HIS THROAT

82. **Jumbles:** CURIO FAMED MANAGE PAROLE
Answer: Something a lot of women are taken in by—A GIRDLE

83. **Jumbles:** NEWLY TEASE FLORAL INNATE
Answer: What she hoped her mother would have—A SON-IN-LAW

84. **Jumbles:** CLUCK QUAIL MARAUD WEAKEN
Answer: What the artist turned cowboy was—QUICK ON THE DRAW

85. **Jumbles:** ANKLE SYLPH BEAVER COMPEL
Answer: A young girl starts to do this when she becomes a teen—PREEN

86. **Jumbles:** CIVIL FINAL DIVERT JUNGLE
Answer: He wouldn't be in such a hurry if he knew he was this—DRIVING TO JAIL

87. **Jumbles:** BRINY ACUTE STUCCO FETISH
Answer: When his wife gave birth to quintuplets, he could hardly believe this—HIS "CENSUS" (senses)

88. **Jumbles:** GLADE NEEDY ENTIRE CANDID
Answer: Where do zombies like to sit when they go to the movies?—DEAD CENTER

89. **Jumbles:** TULIP SAUTE CARPET LAGOON
Answer: What teacher said when he sat on a tack—I GET THE POINT

90. **Jumbles:** SOGGY TAKEN CENSUS BROGUE
Answer: What you'd expect to have for breakfast at a lighthouse—"BEACON" & EGGS

91. **Jumbles:** COUGH ALTAR SAILOR WISELY
Answer: What you might see at a planetarium—AN ALL-STAR SHOW

92. **Jumbles:** FLOOR SHOWY MARTIN PARDON
Answer: What he did every time he bought a suit—HAD A FIT

93. **Jumbles:** LINGO JUICY CEMENT HOMING
Answer: What a lawyer sometimes helps you get—WHAT'S COMING TO HIM

94. **Jumbles:** VOUCH CABIN BLAZER SOOTHE
Answer: What was all that talk down at the garbage dump?—A LOT OF RUBBISH

95. **Jumbles:** LAPEL CREEL TERROR ABRUPT
Answer: What that first tavern in the Arctic was called—THE POLAR BAR

96. **Jumbles:** FRIAR ELDER EITHER HELMET
Answer: What the stag was forced to run for—"DEER" LIFE

97. **Jumbles:** PIANO FIORD NOUGAT SCARCE
Answer: When looking for bargains, you might go there—WHERE THE "AUCTION" IS

98. **Jumbles:** IGLOO PILOT VERSUS UNPACK
Answer: What the broken soft drink machine was—"COIN-IVOROUS"

99. **Jumbles:** RIVET AWFUL SUGARY CHISEL
Answer: What good camouflage is—WISE GUISE

100. **Jumbles:** QUIRE NOISE FLEECE RATHER
Answer: What that great horror film was—"TERROR-IFIC"

101. **Jumbles:** HONEY CRIME GIMLET BYWORD
Answer: What she thought when she switched from high heels to sneakers—"IT'S A BIG LETDOWN"

102. **Jumbles:** BLAZE FORTY TINKLE SPRUCE
Answer: What to do about squeaky furniture wheels—USE "CASTER" OIL

103. **Jumbles:** GROUP ADMIT YEOMAN SUCKLE
Answer: A tiresome person always takes his time doing this—TAKING YOURS

104. **Jumbles:** AGONY ENACT BUCKLE NICELY
Answer: What her companions called that stupid hen—A BIG CLUCK

105. **Jumbles:** EPOCH AGATE MADMAN GALAXY
Answer: What the victim thought when the robber stuffed his mouth with a dirty cloth—"THAT'S AN OLD GAG"

106. **Jumbles:** LOVER WINCE TYPHUS UNLESS
Answer: A scandalmonger is most happy when she confesses this—THE SINS OF OTHERS

107. **Jumbles:** IMPEL ABATE SECOND OFFSET
Answer: Jokes are always improved when they're this—TOLD BY THE BOSS

108. **Jumbles:** EXACT FLAME MOSAIC HARROW
Answer: What do ghosts eat for breakfast?—SCREAM OF WHEAT

109. **Jumbles:** SNACK CHIDE LACKEY FORMAT
Answer: What she called him when he welshed on his promise to buy her a new mink—A FINK

110. **Jumbles:** ROBIN ELOPE CYMBAL POROUS
Answer: Seems to grow abundantly in this yard—A BUMPER CROP

111. **Jumbles:** NEWSY GOURD SUBTLY FIDDLE
Answer: What the young couple called their drive to lovers lane—A "BUSS" RIDE

112. **Jumbles:** COWER PAYEE DENTAL FEDORA
Answer: She became the chief artist because she was—TOP "DRAW-ER"

113. **Jumbles:** SKIMP AGATE FASTEN MORBID
Answer: How the yacht race left the nervous skipper—TIED UP IN KNOTS

114. **Jumbles:** PRIME WRATH INSIST MORGUE
Answer: What the angry field hands called their grievances—GRIPES OF WRATH

115. **Jumbles:** CHASM ROUSE NESTLE GRISLY
Answer: What carelessness sometimes leads to—CARLESSNESS

116. **Jumbles:** PAGAN CHOKE CHARGE MUFFIN
Answer: Why she kept changing her wallpaper—IT WAS A HANG-UP

117. **Jumbles:** MERGE BYLAW MEASLY PLURAL
Answer: Why they stayed away from the boss—HE WAS SURLY EARLY

118. **Jumbles:** LOFTY LIBEL CARBON STUCCO
Answer: What the amateur rocketeers called themselves—A "BOOSTER" CLUB

119. **Jumbles:** BRAVO VIXEN COOPER MALADY
Answer: What the two physicians were called—A "PARADOX" (pair o' docs)

120. **Jumbles:** REARM HOARD DISOWN OUTING
Answer: What were the little cowpokes doing at the corral?—THEY WERE HORSIN' AROUND

121. **Jumbles:** DIRTY JOINT BEETLE SALOON
Answer: What the stadium was filled with when the home team won—"TIERS" OF JOY

122. **Jumbles:** IRATE LOWLY INTAKE ABACUS
Answer: What the losing gambler did—BLEW HIS STACK

123. **Jumbles:** TULLE FATAL HEIFER PLAQUE
Answer: What the apple picker thought his job was—"FRUIT-FULL"

124. **Jumbles:** LINGO INKED JOBBER SUGARY
Answer: What the corrupt banker did for the circus—HE JUGGLED THE BOOKS

125. **Jumbles:** BASSO UNCAP TIPTOE DURESS
Answer: What the space school dropouts called themselves—"ASTRO-NOTS"

126. **Jumbles:** WAGER GROUP MAKEUP CRAYON
Answer: What a pulp mill manager never runs out of—PAPER WORK

127. **Jumbles:** PECAN QUOTA GROUCH SCHEME
Answer: What you might call the director of the Western play—A STAGE COACH

128. **Jumbles:** NOISE FENCE PONCHO SEXTON
Answer: It's helpful to have this when you want something at City Hall—CONNECTIONS

129. **Jumbles:** TAWNY RIGOR WHINNY RENEGE
Answer: When the alarm clock fell in the water it was—"WRINGING" WET

130. **Jumbles:** AGENT MOUNT CHEERY MISFIT
Answer: How unsuccessful archeologists often find their careers—IN "RUINS"

131. **Jumbles:** WRING PICKY OPAQUE UTMOST
Answer: If he was going to buy another horse, he would have to—PONY UP

132. **Jumbles:** HOIST PRONE GLANCE HAIRDO
Answer: The new jumbo jet was—IN "PLANE" SIGHT

133. **Jumbles:** FAINT GLADE SESAME VORTEX
Answer: When he answered questions about all the touchdowns scored against his team, he—GOT DEFENSIVE

134. **Jumbles:** MURKY GRIME COMEDY STENCH
Answer: The technician forgot to change the android's positronic brain. He needed a—"RE-MIND-ER"

135. **Jumbles:** CRAWL MOUND PREFER IMPOSE
Answer: After finishing the 18th hole, they stopped to eat a—ONE-COURSE MEAL

136. **Jumbles:** ALIAS NOVEL HARDLY BEHAVE
Answer: The newscaster used makeup to cover his—HEAD LINES

137. **Jumbles:** ONION THEME MUTATE REFUSE
Answer: The polygraph test was the—MOMENT OF TRUTH

138. **Jumbles:** RANCH PROUD LAWFUL OUTLET
Answer: The police searched the building because it was—WARRANTED

139. **Jumbles:** BRAWL CATCH GALLOP STICKY
Answer: Dracula enjoyed going to the Transylvania circus to watch the—"ACRO-BATS"

140. **Jumbles:** BRICK LAUGH NATIVE BETRAY
Answer: The non-smokers met with the smokers to—CLEAR THE AIR

141. **Jumbles:** FRUIT SUSHI DREDGE EXPIRE
Answer: When the winds abruptly died, all the kite flyers were—"DIS-GUSTED"

142. **Jumbles:** TREND SHOVE ROSIER FIBULA
Answer: The successful arm wrestler was winning prize money—HAND OVER FIST

143. **Jumbles:** VALVE ELECT FLEECE ABACUS
Answer: You know it's autumn when the—LEAVES LEAVE

144. **Jumbles:** MUSTY POKER TATTLE COUGAR
Answer: The vacationing book lovers were on the—SAME PAGE

145. **Jumbles:** EXPEL GIDDY PASTRY BOTHER
Answer: King Kong went to the New York City fruit stand in search of a—BIG APPLE

146. **Jumbles:** ROUND RUGBY SMOOCH BOTHER
Answer: The clown wasn't laughing after he broke his—HUMERUS

147. **Jumbles:** FLASH NEEDY ROTATE BARREN
Answer: The selection of new glasses was right—BEFORE HER EYES

148. **Jumbles:** ADAGE FLUID PEANUT OBJECT
Answer: After the horse's girlfriend broke up with him, he had a—LONG FACE

149. **Jumbles:** AWFUL ENACT OBLIGE SPRAIN
Answer: He had trouble finding tenants for his Death Valley apartments, even with their—LOW RENTS

150. **Jumbles:** ONION TIGHT ABACUS PELVIC
Answer: To get rid of last season's fashions, the boutique had this type of sale—A "CLOTHES-OUT"

151. **Jumbles:** GRIME IGLOO HURRAY KARATE
Answer: The barbershop had been in his family for years and it was his turn to run it…It was his—"HAIR-ITAGE"

152. **Jumbles:** FLUKE AUDIO GOBBLE BESIDE
Answer: The usher at the theater wanted to be an author, so he wrote a—GUIDE BOOK

153. **Jumbles:** FADED GRAND USEFUL HELMET
Answer: He was able to afford his new landscaping after making so much money in his—HEDGE FUND

154. **Jumbles:** PRICE MILKY AIRWAY CLEVER
Answer: After his heart surgery, the marathon runner was happy to once again be a—PACE-MAKER

155. **Jumbles:** CLOUT APPLY HYBRID BOUNCE
Answer: There were no eggs in the henhouse because they had been—POACHED

156. **Jumbles:** DIRTY HUMID INLAND BUFFET
Answer: While watching their kids play soccer, the parents had a—FIELD DAY

157. **Jumbles:** WEARY YOUNG SUBDUE EXPOSE
Answer: When he wasn't working as a mild-mannered reporter, Clark Kent was—SUPER BUSY

158. **Jumbles:** TOKEN DOUSE GENTRY TIRADE
Answer: The king and queen of the caribou were—"REIGN"-DEER

159. **Jumbles:** APRON BRAVO LOCALE GLITZY
Answer: When King George read the Declaration of Independence, he found it to be—REVOLTING

160. **Jumbles:** ALPHA FRONT DIVERT SUDDEN
Answer: She adored Bruce Willis and always would, because she was a—DIE-HARD FAN

161. **Jumbles:** SKINNY FINALE ADJUST EXPOSE VACANT CRUTCH
Answer: The bank's grand opening suffered from—LACK OF INTEREST

162. **Jumbles:** SPRAWL TRAUMA SPRUNG TOWARD INDIGO ENGAGE
Answer: The church's relocation required—AN ORGAN TRANSPLANT

163. **Jumbles:** REFUSE ACQUIT ABSORB VALLEY HUDDLE UNPACK
Answer: The limbo champion was one—AN UNDERACHIEVER

164. **Jumbles:** BATTER AVENUE ACTUAL PICKET SAFARI MOSAIC
Answer: The flight attendant was starting to feel the—CABIN PRESSURE

165. **Jumbles:** ZENITH ASTHMA EXCEED OBLONG ASSURE WRITER
Answer: Hunting on a windy day allowed them to—SHOOT THE BREEZE

166. **Jumbles:** SMOOTH ACTUAL BARREN PRANCE FICKLE WHEEZE
Answer: What they would end up calling the humpback king and queen's son—THE PRINCE OF "WHALES"

167. **Jumbles:** SQUAWK BUDGET EQUATE MUFFIN INSIST GIGGLE
Answer: When the beetle's wife asked him to take out the garbage for the third time, he said this—QUIT BUGGING ME

168. **Jumbles:** INFECT ANYHOW INFLUX REFUSE GARLIC SHODDY
Answer: When they counted the number of dads at the cookout, they ended up with—FATHER FIGURES

169. **Jumbles:** INJECT WORTHY WEAPON DRENCH ANTHEM EXCESS
Answer: The new spa featured these—WINDOW TREATMENTS

170. **Jumbles:** GLOSSY GROUND JOCKEY AGENCY INTENT ASSIGN
Answer: You get so many cards during the holidays because it's—GREETINGS SEASON

171. **Jumbles:** ASTRAY DECODE HUNTER HAWKER MAYHEM CRAVAT
Answer: Cold eggs and lukewarm coffee can result in—"HEATED" REMARKS

172. **Jumbles:** NUANCE JAGUAR PHYSIC OUTFIT INDICT BOLERO
Answer: What the actor needed for the fishing scene—A "CASTING" DIRECTOR

173. **Jumbles:** HEARSE ATOMIC TRYING CLERGY BANGLE HOURLY
Answer: When the parsley farmer didn't pay his debt, he faced—"GARNISH-MENT"

174. **Jumbles:** PLACID KITTEN BESIDE SINFUL FIESTA CLAUSE
Answer: What the exercise club lost when business slumped—FISCAL FITNESS

175. **Jumbles:** STRONG POISON GOODLY BELLOW SAFARI IMPUGN
Answer: When the boss stopped by, the hard-working printer made a—GOOD "IMPRESSION"

176. **Jumbles:** AGHAST UNLESS RATHER CALMLY AFLOAT COMMON
Answer: Often found in "the classroom"—SCHOOLMASTER

177. **Jumbles:** EMBALM DUGOUT JIGGER GENTLE GAMBIT INDICT
Answer: Why he decided to eat the whole pie—TO INDULGE THE BULGE

178. **Jumbles:** DEMURE RELISH QUARTZ OUTLET HECTIC PARITY
Answer: What he did when he gave Mom a big hug—PUT THE "SQUEEZE" ON HER

179. **Jumbles:** ORIOLE POLISH HEARSE STUDIO WORTHY MORGUE
Answer: Wearing a tie to a fancy casino doesn't mean you won't do this—LOSE YOUR SHIRT

180. **Jumbles:** DOOMED SNUGLY LAWFUL KNOTTY STOLID JINGLE
Answer: Their extended good-bye turned into a—SO LONG "SO-LONG"